Codependent No More

Stop Codependency

It's time to start loving yourself

By

Shell Teri

Table of Contents

Introduction

"You yourself, as much as anybody in the entire universe, deserve your love and affection." – **Buddha**

Everyone believes that relationships are a two-way street. There should be mutual understanding, benefits, sacrifice and joy.

If you are at a place where you are the one shouldering all the burden, it's high time you cut your losses. Codependency is such a one-way journey that you should think of freeing yourself from.

I started this journey, when I found the courage to get away from the stifling influence of my now ex-husband. He was ten years older than me. I was deeply in love with him and we had two daughters.

Even before our marriage, if I remember it right, from the day we met he decided how everything would go. From the house where we lived to managing our finances, he pulled all the strings. Initially I thought it was sweet of him to be so possessive.

But soon it dawned on me that he had built a cage around me. Each and everything I did was under his control. I couldn't meet my friends and he was against me working. But I thank God that I was at least stubborn on having my job, as it helped me move on after I left him.

After a very frustrating, demeaning and destructive decade of living with him, I finally broke away from the vicious circle of codependency. While the liberating journey had its ups and downs and sometimes, I felt it downright impossible to move on, I don't regret any part of it.

In fact, I see it as my awakening phase. I now have everything I dreamed of, but was not within my reach, because I was reluctant to come out of the tangled web of codependency.

But now that I have emerged and find how beautiful life can be, I want to share my experience and thoughts on dealing with codependency and being free of it once and for all.

Codependent relationship is one where you find you are sacrificing your friendships, responsibilities, happiness and your own identity. Such an unhealthy relationship can batter your self-esteem and make you lose sight of yourself. It is a lethal situation that you should put in all your efforts to get rid of.

Now the trouble with codependency is you never acknowledge that you are living in a codependent relationship. You wear yourself out trying to please your partner seeking reassurance and love, which your partner will never give to you.

If you worry all day thinking about your relationship and keep finding excuses for the impossible behavior of your partner, you are cheating yourself in believing the relationship will work out.

There are other factors that can play significant part in increasing the codependency like addiction to drugs, alcohol etc.

And codependency is a complicated phenomenon that needs to be dealt with properly, if you want to emerge from it and regain your self-esteem and live your life as you deserve.

This book is my effort to give to others who are in a similar codependent relationship and struggling to be free of it. You will find the why, what, when, how and where of resolving your dilemma in my book.

Not only will you understand about what codependency is and how to be free of it, you will also learn what you need to do to heal yourself and get on the path of self-realization, joy and happiness.

After all everyone deserves to be happy. It is just a matter of having the courage to grab yours. I am sure my book will help in giving the impetus needed to free yourself from codependency. Read on to know how you can start on your journey of self-discovery and bliss.

PART I: The Dormant Phase

If you are in a one sided and emotionally destructive relationship for a long time and doing nothing about it, chances are that you are not aware of it. This is what I call as dormant phase.

You make yourself believe that it is natural to sacrifice your needs over that of your partner. However, when you end up taking the entire brunt of a relationship, it can take a big toll on your emotional and physical health.

It can wreak havoc with the interpersonal relationships you have with others and the relationship with yourself.

Here is a quiz you should take:

- Are you having a difficult time uttering the word "no"?
- Do you feel the constant urge to take care of those around you?
- Are you emotionally reactive?
- Do you have poor limits on the extent of work you do for others?
- Do you keep going over your mistakes feeling that you could have done something to avoid it
- Are you a people pleaser?
- Do you confuse love with pity?
- Are you afraid of being abandoned?
- Do you have intimacy issues?
- Do you find it difficult to communicate your thoughts honestly?

If your answer to many or all of the above questions is yes, then you are in a codependent relationship. Most often you are in such a relationship because you fail to acknowledge that you are having problems.

You do not talk about them nor do you confront your partner with it. You try to repress your emotions and ignore your own needs. You just survive each day developing behaviors that help you keep in denial and ignorance. You do not communicate your angst and do not trust.

But this is just a phase where you are an onlooker of your own life. It is time you took the initiative to see your relationship as it is.

You need to put your own desires, needs and yourself first. To achieve this, you have to first know what a codependent relationship is, how it develops and in what ways it can affect your emotional and physical wellbeing.

To download the free guide copy the link below in your browser window

https://bit.ly/35KjsZb

Chapter 1: Defining a Codependent Relationship

Codependency is a dysfunctional and one-sided relationship between two people, where one person disproportionately sacrifices his or her needs and wants, and makes excuses for the reckless and abusive behavior of the other person.

Experts say it is a learned behavior that is passed through generations. It is a behavioral and emotional condition that impairs your ability to have a healthy and mutually satisfying relationship. Most often it stems from watching or imitating a family member or members who exhibit a similar behavior.

Codependency is also called as relationship addiction.

This is because codependent people tend to be attracted to an emotionally destructive, abusive and one-sided relationship.

Behavior of Codependent People

Codependents mostly have self-esteem issues. They believe that they can feel better only by catering to the needs of those around them.

They cannot be themselves. In some cases, codependent people try to make themselves feel better by taking drugs, nicotine or alcohol and soon become addicted.

A few can develop compulsive obsessive disorders like indiscriminate sexual relations, gambling, workaholism and more.

It is not that codependent behavior is fully destructive at least in the beginning. You start with good intention of taking care of the needs of your partner or a relative. You let the other individual define your happiness and mood and even your identity. Soon it turns into a defeating and compulsive one.

Personality Traits in Codependent Relationships

In general, codependent relationship involves two different personalities:

1. A passive person who cannot decide for themselves
2. A dominant person who derives satisfaction and reward from wielding control over the passive person and deciding on how the other person lives.

While controlling behavior and jealousy are big issues to confront, the situation takes a turn for the worse, when one person exploits the other emotionally or financially.

Enabling Trait in Codependency

Enabling is a surefire sign that the codependency is becoming unhealthy. It is a behavior developed to reduce the escalating tension triggered by the problematic habits of his or her partner. Healthy relationships rarely have enabling behavior.

Some examples of enabling behavior include:

- A wife can end up making excuses for the abusive behavior of her husband
- A mother may cover for her delinquent son.
- A person may repeatedly bail out a partner or keep giving another chance for the partner to change
- Turn a blind eye to the controlling behavior of a spouse
- Accepting excuses
- Volunteering to resolve the issue, even if the person did not cause it

The issue becomes serious when such patterns become repetitive taking you on a destructive path. You become dependent on the unhealthy relationship. You thrive on being needed and feel it as a reward.

Soon it becomes a vicious cycle where you find it impossible to come out of. You start feeling like a victim unable to find a way to veer off the path you have set yourself on.

The Childhood Connection

Codependency is mostly spoken of in connection with people who are suffering some kind of addiction such as substance abuse or alcohol. The persons who support such addicts are called codependent as they enable them to continue with their inappropriate behavior sacrificing their own needs and happiness.

Codependency has been linked to not just this type of sacrificial trait but to childhood conditions that laid the foundation to codependency.

Psychology experts believe that the traits for codependency develop very early on in life. Gradually the person involved gets lured by challenging relationships in personal and professional life.

In fact, any relationship they have at work, with family or friends is potentially rife with difficulty.

Some traits in a codependent person can give definite clues as to the presence of the behavior. Most often a codependent keeps on talking about his or her partner or family member who is being an influential person in their life. The conversations that happen are mostly about the feelings of the other person.

Why does this happen?

This is because codependents are immune to their own feelings. Their entire focus is on the other person's wellbeing that they fail to see how it is affecting their own mental and physical state.

By allowing the other individual to control you, use you or hurt you repeatedly, you are falling deep into the destructive relationship.

In short, codependent people generally show a behavioral pattern that is problematic, consistent and impacts directly on their emotional health.

The condition robs them of the ability to find fulfillment in the relationship.

Some important signs of codependency you can recognize include excessive:

- Controlling
- Caretaking
- Preoccupation with things and people outside of oneself

Is codependency as bad as it seems?

To be truthful, all codependent relationships do not take a downward spiral. There can be some give and take along with codependency even in healthy relationships. For instance, if a wife seeks advice from her husband while making a major decision, it is a reasonable one.

But if you purposely seek out or maintain or feed off unhealthy behavior, it can turn bad for your wellbeing. The relationship is mainly built on a power imbalance where the taker is in favor, while the giver continues to give without receiving anything from the taker.

There is imbalance in the giving and taking, thus violating the essential aspects of close and healthy relationships. This is because instead of being interdependent and equitable, the relationship is enmeshed and imbalanced.

The most significant part of a codependent relationship is that the affected partner is loyal to the other in spite of the stress they are under.

In a Journal of Substance Abuse study, the characteristics of codependent women included control, rescue orientation, change orientation, exaggerated responsibility, and worth dependency, while for men, it showed just two of the traits, namely exaggerated responsibility and control.

Regardless of how codependency is defined, the gist of it is that it is unhealthy and has lasting effect on your emotional and physical state. You can end up leading a poor quality of life than other people.

Chapter 2: How Codependency Develops

Codependency is often rooted in childhood, wherein the emotions of the child are punished or ignored. Such emotional neglect can result in the child having low self-esteem and shame, and the child may believe that their needs aren't worth attending to.

Typically, this occurs when one or both the parents aren't able to fulfill their roles as guardians. This may require the child to perform deeds that are beyond their developmental ability. For instance, if a parent is too drunk to cook, the child may have to learn to cook lest the family go hungry.

Often, a child may have to step in and fulfill the role of the adult or even be expected to care for the parent. Domestic violence at home may also turn the child into a confidante. Furthermore, if a parent is narcissistic, the parent may demand the child to give them praise and comfort.

However, since children are not grown-ups, fulfilling the role of the adult can take up all their effort. Focusing on keeping their household in working conditions might lead them to ignore their own needs.

This may lead them to associate their role as a caregiver with feelings of control and stability. Although such behaviors may be necessary in childhood, they are not so adaptive.

Codependency can, in fact, prevent people from developing stable relationships.

Codependency also arises in a relationship with a person that has an addiction. Here too, the person with codependency takes over the role of the 'caretaker.' She/he may handle the partner's finances, chores, and may cover for issues outside their relationship.

For instance, the partner may skip work due to substance abuse and the codependent person may call the boss on their behalf claiming that their partner is sick. Though the caregiver may help the partner out of a desire for help, she/he inadvertently ends up supporting the addiction.

When the caretaker saves the partner from the consequences of the addiction, the partner loses the motivation to change. Without any change, the addiction may get worse.

Such a relationship can also harm the caretaker as the codependent person may neglect their own needs to care for the addicted partner.

Codependency also develops when one lives in an abusive relationship or household. Codependent behaviors develop by countering the feelings that result from emotional abuse. For instance, one may cater to the needs of the addicted person in order to feel needed; another may earn gratitude by foregoing their own needs to cater to others; while others still may feel empowered by 'saving' others.

A codependent person may feel responsible for saving the partner. In case, the partner suffers from mental health conditions, she/he may try to 'heal' them with care. But, love isn't enough to tackle mental health condition and professional help is necessary.

Many codependent households may think that by keeping their problems private, they are protecting their family. However, allowing the partner to continue with abuse only ends up causing harm to the other family members. Not reporting child abuse also makes one an accomplice, which brings about legal ramifications.

Codependent parents might try to live vicariously through their children. As some parents protect their children from all hardship, others try to control the child's life so they live up to the parents' definition of success. Such behaviors increase the risk of children becoming codependent.

As children explore the world on their own, they develop a sense of independence. However, when parents end up making all their decisions for them, the child may grow up ignoring their own desires. Again, they may learn to value other people's approval above their own needs.

Such effects can last for years. Codependent children lack self-confidence and struggle in making decisions as adults. Instead, they look for relationships in which their partner has all the power and make their decisions for them.

If no intervention takes place, this cycle of codependence may continue into the next generation. There is a subconscious connection to becoming codependent. If a parent is abused or neglected and is unwilling to overcome codependency, the behaviors and personality traits may transfer to their children.

There are certain behavioral patterns that are similar across codependent families and households. These are as follows:

- Becoming a caretaker – This happens especially when you are forced to fulfill the roles of your parents.

- Learning that people who tell you they love you actually end up hurting you – As your codependent family hurt you physically or emotionally, you tend to find friends and lovers that continue that trend into adulthood.

- Becoming a people-pleaser – Pleasing other people is a way to feel in control. Since you don't speak or disagree out of fear, you gain self-worth only through giving unconditionally.

- Struggling with boundaries – Nobody taught you how to maintain healthy boundaries. So now either your boundaries are too weak or too rigid.

- Feeling guilty – Your inability to 'fix' your family leads you to feeling guilty even though it is illogical.

- Feeling alone and untrustworthy – People hurt and betrayed you in the past, which makes you cynical of their motives even when they are your close friends and lovers. Many would even seek solitude and be alone rather than form meaningful relationships.

This is how codependency starts to develop. Living with codependency often feels like operating with a false self. It takes a lot of effort to recover from codependency, and much more to even see through it.

If one has been brought up in an environment of codependency, it may feel normal to be this way. This is why it can be an overly cumbersome task to make someone see their codependent behavior.

Once someone tries to look for help for their codependent behavior, they realize how much of their lives they have lost. Such realization is often followed by anger at the injustice of such a behavioral pattern.

People may realize that they had not had a childhood, missed important events in their lives, or weren't allowed to talk about their problems because of the secrecy surrounding their codependent families. Such things and many more, may resurface.

Anger, then, becomes a positive sign, since this means that codependent people are reclaiming their individuality and dignity, thus breaking the codependent cycle.

Chapter 3: Codependency in Marriage Relationships

In marriage, codependency occurs when one partner is so heavily invested in the relationship that it is impossible for them to imagine a life without their partner. Regardless of how their partner treats them, they are willing to endure it all just to stay in the relationship.

It's a sort of an addiction where they think that the partner would not be able to live without them or that they themselves would not survive the end of the relationship.

Codependency in marriage may feel like you've lost sight of your own life as a result of your unwavering focus on your partner. It may seem contradictory to the belief that one should care for one's spouse during marriage.

But, in fact, codependency is blatantly obvious when someone cares too much about managing and controlling their spouse, and in turn, loses sight of controlling and managing one's own life and behavior. In both cases, the unhealthy imbalance is a result of codependency.

Most, if not all, codependent behavior sprouts from low self-esteem and can often go unrecognized in the person exhibiting such behavior. Such a behavior interferes with the relationship and spells doom for both individuals.

The balance of power and opportunity for decision making and growth is the hallmark of a healthy relationship. However, when one person decides to take over, make up rules and take charge of the relationship for any reason, imbalance occurs.

This can be either out of a sense of having no choice in the matter or because they do not care for or respect what their partner thinks, and the other person simply lets it happen in order to keep peace.

When two people, on the other hand, are able to freely and openly discuss their dreams and goals while helping each other reach those goals, a healthy relationship ensues.

So, how can one know if they're in a codependent marriage?

Watch out for the following signs:

- Are you incapable of finding satisfaction in your life outside of your marriage?

- Are you living with your partner despite their unhealthy behaviors towards you?

- Are you prioritizing your partner's mental, emotional, and physical health over yours?

If your answer to all of the aforementioned questions is yes, then you might be in an unhealthy, codependent marriage. If people around you provide you with the feedback that you are too dependent on your partner, or you feel conflicted when you have a desire to be more independent, then it is safe to assume that you are in a codependent relationship.

One of the defining emotions for people in a codependent relationship is anxiety. This is because they spend a great deal of energy and time trying to either change their partner or conform to their wishes.

As a result, people in codependent relationship may be burned out, exhausted, and start to neglect other relationships. Similarly, if they are the ones that have all the reins of the relationship, they can prevent their partners from growing, learning, and achieving their own life goals.

In many cultures, such a sacrificial and martyr-like role of unconditional giving and codependency is completely acceptable. This is more so the case for women than men, but it definitely doesn't make it a healthy phenomenon. Instead, it only gives credibility to what is inherently flawed.

It is important to spend some time apart from your partner to recognize any burgeoning emotions that may point towards codependency.

For instance, if spending time with relatives, friends, and family makes you feel anxious, helpless, or low in confidence, and you're longing for the support of your partner, then it is safe to assume that you're living in a codependent relationship.

Some codependents are also suffering from addictions. They may have no sense of boundaries, while others may have such thick walls around them that no one can get in. Whatever the cause may be, codependency leads to emotional dysfunction that affects all areas of life.

Recognizing imbalance in relationships can allow couples to take reasonable steps during the decision-making process. It is also an important factor in settling agreements fairly. Studies show that if couples reach agreements that worked out carefully to create balance, conflict arises.

When working through a divorce, an important thing is to learn what belongs to each person. It is not only a matter of debts and assets, but also of emotional components.

If one of the partners says they are fine with whatever just to get through the process, perhaps it is time to slow things down and reassess balance. Conversely, if someone is answering all the questions and guiding the decision making process, it may be yet another sign of imbalance.

Other indicators of codependency in marriage may be much more nuanced and subtle. In such situations, a good mediator, attorney, or facilitator can help sort out the issues before a settlement is signed off.

Many a time, codependent behavior may look like sacrifice in the name of true love. But if it comes at the expense of one partner, then it arises from a sense of low self-esteem and it must always be questioned. Both individuals should be fully responsible for their own decisions.

It is important for people in codependent marriages to

Take care of one's own needs

Truly love themself

Avoid being narcissistic or selfish but rather maintain a healthy balance.

When one expects reciprocity and respect from their partners, it shouldn't be realistic. Instead, this is what defines love. But allowing your partner to hurt you says much more about your own sense of self than it says about them.

Though it is true that many types of relationship can be codependent, one cannot overlook the fact that it can arise out of one's own personality traits. That is why one should be cautious not to wave the moniker of codependency like a flag.

Recovering from codependent behavioral traits can not only save your marriage, but also allow you to change your life for the better in ways unimaginable. This shows that the only way to change the nature of your relationship and your response to it is to change yourself.

Chapter 4: Codependency dynamics: Relationship problems that can trigger or exacerbate codependency

Codependency is not limited to your relationships but is tied to all areas of life. Though it is not entirely separated from how one was brought up, one's current behaviors have a lot of impact on the dynamics of codependency.

Such things as being addicted to a substance, abusing or being at the receiving end of abuse, unhealthy parenting, and caregiving can all trigger or exacerbate codependency.

In order to understand how each of these elements affects codependency, it is important to isolate them and scrutinize each one of them separately.

Addiction

Codependency might happen when one of the partners has some kind of addiction. This addiction can be of substance abuse, relationships, work, shopping, sex, food, or gambling. In such a case, the other partner becomes a caretaker of the addicted partner. The caretaker handles all the household chores as well as finances.

Moreover, in case the addiction causes problems outside the relationship, the caretaker covers for the addicted partner. For instance, if the partner has an addiction to alcohol, then they might skip work due to it. Then, the codependent partner might call their partner's boss and tell them that their partner is not feeling well.

The caretaker helps the partner just to save them. However, due to these repeated rescue attempts, the other partner continues with their addiction as they know that their partner will save them from the consequences of their addiction. This makes them lose the motivation to change or seek professional help, thus exacerbating the addiction. They go forward on the destructive path and become more dependent on the caretaker.

Nevertheless, the caretaker is not responsible for their partner's addiction. Even though their codependent behavior might contribute to the addicted partner refusing treatment, it's not the sole cause of it. A person cannot force someone else to go to a rehabilitation center.

This kind of a relationship can harm the caretaker as well. The codependent partner ignores their own requirements and desires in order to care for their partner. And, these codependent habits can aggravate with time. Moreover, the caretaker might not get treatment for their own mental health issues.

Abuse

Codependency might also develop from being in an abusive relationship or living in an abusive home. Abuse can be sexual, emotional, or physical. Emotional abuse might make people feel insignificant and trivial.

In order to offset these feelings, codependent behavior can start to grow. Such a person might take on the role of a caretaker for a person having some addiction so as to feel wanted. Or, they might want to get praise by catering to the needs of others and ignoring their own requirements.

Saving others makes the caretaker feel important and empowered. The codependent person might feel responsible for the abusive person. In case, the abusive person's mental health issue is not treated, the codependent person might think that their love and care will heal them. However, mental health issues cannot be healed by just love; they require professional treatment and care.

People in codependent homes might feel like they are saving their family by not reporting the mental condition and keeping it private. However, this might worsen the mental health of the abusive person and thus cause harm to other family members living in the house.

Moreover, by not reporting domestic abuse, you help the person committing the offense, leading to legal consequences.

Parenting

Codependent parents try to live via their kids. Some of them protect their children from all adversities in life and others control their kids so that they can grow up and fulfill their parent's definition of success. This might lead to codependency behavior in such children.

When the child is allowed to take their own decisions, make their own plans, and explore the world, they become independent. However, when parents take all decisions on behalf of their child, the child might neglect their own requirements. Moreover, such children might seek approval for whatever they do and put this approval above their own desires.

This can make the child codependent for several years. Such kids would not be able to make their own decisions and lack confidence. Therefore, such children might look for relationships where the other partner takes control and holds power. This cycle of codependency might go on for another generation, if it's left untreated.

Caregiving

Caretakers treat their loved ones throughout their life for a disability, or a chronic physical or mental ailment. For instance, they may help them daily to bathe or move from one place to another. They put in their whole energy and attention on the addicted or ill person, while sacrificing their own needs.

The caretaker takes on the role of a martyr and become a benefactor to an ill person. Such people place the other person's safety, welfare, and health above their own and thus disregard their own desires, needs, and sense of self.

Caregiving is quite hard on its own and codependency further complicates it. However, you might be confused as to whether you have become codependent or are just a caregiver. This is different in different situations. However, if you see the below-mentioned signs in you, then it's time for you to get help.

- **Trying to control all decisions of your loved ones:** If you want your dear ones to do everything according to your wish, then you might be in trouble. Taking a decision when it comes to the health or safety of that person is fine. However, when you want to take even the smallest decisions of your loved ones, such as what kind of clothes they wear, then you are codependent.
- **Spending all your time with your dear ones:** Caregiving takes a lot of energy and time. Still, it's crucial to take some rest and have a social life apart from your dear ones. If you don't do so, you will be left exhausted and become resentful.
- **Convincing your loved ones, you are their sole caretaker:** You might think of other caregivers as your opponents or discourage your dear ones from being independent. This is because you want to feel needed by the other person, resulting in feelings of satisfaction and contentment. If this is the same with you, then you are codependent.

So, these are the primary relationship issues that can trigger or worsen codependency.

The problem with codependent people is that they do not accept that they are facing such issues. They don't confront or talk about their issues. This leads to blocking their own emotions and neglecting their own needs.

Such people become survivors by developing behaviors that aid them to avoid, ignore, or deny their difficult emotions. Moreover, they don't touch, feel, and trust. They just detach themselves from others, which inhibits their emotional as well as identity development.

Codependency can cause a lot of anxiety on both you as well as your dear ones. Therefore, it's crucial to address codependent behavior and enhance your relationship. You can start by communicating with your loved one or setting proper boundaries between you and them. This can make a taxing situation better.

Chapter 5: The negative impact of codependent relationships

Codependency is not good for a person's overall well-being. In fact, its symptoms can get worse, if the behavior is not treated. Being in a codependent relationship can lead to many dire issues and you might not even be aware of them.

Codependent people generally have low self-respect and strong feelings of shame. This can lead to emotional distress and anxiety on a regular basis. Unresolved codependency can also result in drug addiction, eating disorders, as well as alcoholism.

Such people rarely seek medical care and continue living in stressful situations. Due to this, the person can have social insecurity, which can further result in social anxiety and disorders related to stress, such as depression.

Codependency can also have negative side effects on your body, such as ulcers, high blood pressure, respiratory issues, headaches, heart problems, etc. Thus, codependency is unhealthy for your physical, mental, as well as emotional well-being.

According to studies, codependent relationships have the following negative impacts.

Depression: Lack of trust in yourself and others might make you feel depressive. Moreover, you don't share your feelings with anyone or defend your opinion since you fear that you will be exposed and the other person will leave you. This makes you bottle up all your emotions for a long time period, leading to depression and anxiety.

Anxiety or fear: Codependency might constantly make you feel anxious about your relationship. You will always think about how you can make your partner happy, which will make you restless.

Moreover, a codependent relationship can make you fear your safety as well as the safety of your partner, family, and friends.

Since such people are frequently told that they are unworthy of love and not good enough, they fear that no one will want them and they have to stay alone forever.

The abuser or manipulator uses this fear to keep the codependent person trapped in the relationship, which further augments the feeling of worthlessness in codependent individuals.

Dependent personality: You would want other people to like you so that you can feel good about yourself. This would make you feel important and wanted. Such people are scared of being abandoned or rejected, even if they can function on their own.

Moreover, codependent people might always want to be in a relationship, otherwise, they feel lonely or depressed when they are on their own.

Such people invest so much of their energy and time on the other person in the relationship that they lose sight of themselves and start lacking solitude. This is why codependent people find it difficult to end even an abusive or painful relationship. And, hence, they feel trapped in the relationship.

Substance abuse: In order to avoid and cover up their emotions, people might get addicted to abusing substances. The codependent partner might abuse substances in order to get close to their addicted partner. Or else, the addicted partner might pressurize the codependent person to drink alcohol or use drugs.

Low self-esteem: A codependent relationship might make you lose your self-respect and feel worthless and unloved. This means you will constantly compare yourself with others and think that you are not good enough, along with feelings of guilt and perfectionism.

Moreover, you will depend on meeting your partner's needs and other external reinforcements in order to feel positive self-worth. Due to less confidence, you will not be able to take up any position of leadership in your academic or professional life.

You will feel unlovable outside your relationship and depend on other people's opinions in order to feel positive self-worth.

Controlling nature: You might become controlling due to a codependent relationship. By controlling others, you might feel safe and secure. You would want to control your loved ones so that they behave as per your desires. This makes you feel better.

Additionally, you might become bossy and tell others what they should or should not do. When you give someone advice, you want them to follow your advice. You don't understand boundaries. To control the behavior of others, you might also use tactics like manipulation, guilt, and shame.

Chronic anger: You do not pay heed to your own wants and needs since you are so much focused on ensuring that the other person is alright. And, when you are not personally satisfied over a long term, resentment builds up.

This leads to violent fights and shouting when you reach your saturation point, which negatively impacts both your physical as well as mental health.

Difficulty making decisions: As a codependent person, you might always question your judgment and often check your decision with others. You will start having the strong urge for external validation, that is, to rely on others to tell you your value.

This might make you stay in unhealthy relationships so that you can feel worthwhile, valuable, and lovable. And, when you do not get this external validation, you feel unlovable, inadequate, and defective.

Unstable relationships: Not only your present but also your future relationships will suffer owing to your codependent behavior. You will have unstable relationships due to your anxious and avoidant behavior. Moreover, you would not like getting too close or being alone.

Both of these behaviors lead to unsatisfying relationships. Since you cannot communicate assertively with your partner, you might see closeness with a third person, which could further threaten the stability of your relationship.

People-pleasing: Codependent people value the opinions of others over their own in order to feel loved and wanted. They go to great lengths in order to ensure that the other person has a positive perception of them. Such people cannot say 'no' to others and cannot stand up for themselves throughout their life.

Codependent individuals want to be approved, accepted, and liked. And, if they do not get approval, they feel victimized. They feel that they are not complete without their partner. A codependent relationship might make you ignore your own hobbies, friends, and goals.

Thus, these are some of the negative impacts of codependent relationships. Such relationships not only affect the two partners involved in it, but also others who stay in the same house with these people, including children.

Codependency is a cycle of harmful behavior that is bad for everyone. Such relationships only have a negative effect. They stop the growth of individuals and results in desperation and resentment over time. Codependent relationships eventually destroy lives.

PART II: The Awakening Phase

Most people think they know what codependency is; in fact, they think that it's just being overly dependent on your partner.

However, most of them start realizing what the problem really is when issues start getting so bad that a visit to the therapist becomes necessary. This is when they understand what codependency actually is.

As mentioned above, codependency's textbook definition states it is a type of dysfunction where one partner earns and supports and enables the other's under-achievement, irresponsibility, immaturity, poor mental health, gambling addiction, alcoholism, or drug addiction.

These are the types of people who are always giving away to help the other person become better; they never put their feelings first. Ultimately, all they are left with are exhaustion, frustration, and anger when everything ends.

At times, it might be hard to admit that this problem exists within you. After all, you think that your partner is sick, right?

Since they are the ones suffering from addiction and mental health, why would you anyway think that something is wrong with you?

Of course, codependency is a serious problem as well; it is just as much a sickness as addiction or alcoholism. This can take a serious impact on your life and will leave you wondering when did you turn into a tired and angry person.

You basically suffer in the background of the addicted/sick person. And, the worst aspect here is that you do not even realize it.

You find yourself constantly asking why your partner behaves in a way a normal person does and just stop. You start doubting whether your constant support and love is enough for them to want to do better.

This constant support and love turns into an obsession, and then you want to start controlling everything that your partner does. While you might not have meant for it to happen this way, it does.

These feelings keep on accumulating until you find yourself losing sleep, canceling out on plans, or missing work to help save your partner. You start losing yourself and making excuses for anyone who calls you out on this type of behavior.

Soon, frustration starts manifesting inside and you realize that everything that you have done is only thrown back to your face. People will start calling you a controlling and manipulative individual. These traits are picked up only because you are living with a person who responds to these only.

If you start losing seriousness in everything else, including your own self; others will too. This is the part when you start realizing that control is being taken away from you.

You then start fighting with your partner hoping that he/she will start taking you seriously. If it does not work out, you get sick and depressed, wondering when everything went wrong.

If you are left in the situation, you might end up repeating the cycle. This is because you develop a draw towards people who need your 'fixing.' You feel trapped in this cycle. At times, simply knowing that someone needs your help makes you feel secure.

If you are the one who feels all the above-mentioned urges, it means that you have realized that you are very codependent. Thankfully, realizing the problem is the first step towards rehabilitation. This is your awakening.

Chapter 1: How to find you are in a codependent relationship

Do you put the needs of your partner before you?

Are you making excuses for all the things that your partner does?

Do you feel the need to control the behavior of your partner?

If your answer is yes to the above questions, you may be in a codependent relationship. But these are not the only signs of a codependent relationship.

Since codependence has deep rooted causes, as I have mentioned in the earlier chapters, you may not be aware of being in one. Your codependent attitude may not look anything out of ordinary, if you have been exposed to it from childhood.

On the other hand, in some people the relationship turn will be a sudden one. Whatever be the situation that brought you to such a stage, being aware that you are in such a relationship can help you deal with it head on.

Codependency indicators

A codependent relationship happens when your entire thoughts and actions are focused on your partner, ignoring your own needs and wants.

Codependency can sneak on you when you are vulnerable such as when your partner has some mental illness or is addicted to drugs, alcohol, food, video games or any other related addiction.

It is often difficult to recognize a codependent relationship, as the line between a healthy and codependent relationship is a very fine one. When crossed there will be severe consequences to bear.

In truth, a codependent relationship is an intense one with too many highs and lows. You may try to extricate yourself from it, but find you are drawn to the relationship again and again.

As a codependent, you will expend so much energy on making your partner happy, comfortable and satisfied that the relationship will look like your whole world. And the reason why many are not aware of their codependent state is because they confuse it with love.

Here are a few situations that will show you in high definition clarity how seriously in trouble you are.

You are in an unbalanced relationship

Codependency is an unhealthy relationship where one partner keeps on giving, while the other keeps on receiving. In other words, it is an unbalanced relationship.

While it is true that you cannot expect the balance to be perfect in a relationship even in a healthy one, there is a gross shift in balance here.

For a healthy partnership, any giving on your part should be reciprocated, which does not happen in a codependent one.

Absorbing your partner's pain

When you are in a relationship, your partner's struggles and pain will affect you and it is natural to empathize with them. However, if you start taking on their burdens as your own, it indicates codependency.

Instead of being supportive and listening to your partner, if you make your partner's troubles your own, you will soon feel too exhausted to think about anything else.

 And the worst part of this situation is, it is difficult to help you when you are in such a bad situation.

Constant need to bail out

Janet liked the idea of rescuing her boyfriend whenever he got into trouble due to his drug addiction. She thought that her solid support would make him see the wrong of his ways and make him change.

Although this may sound romantic, such behavior actually points to codependency. Rather than Janet helping her boyfriend to get out of his drug addiction, she turns into an enabler.

Ignorance is not always bliss

Kate and her husband did not always see eye to eye on many things. But Kate loved her husband and tried to let things slide, when he got angry with her. While this can prevent things from escalating beyond control, if this happens all the time, brushing it off is not good.

There is a big gap between the partner who ignores the insulting attitude of her spouse and the husband continuing with his unreliable and harsh attitude.

Healthy relationships are all about responsibility. Both partners should be responsible for their emotional state and how it affects their relationship.

Paranoia and Justification

Melanie tried to be what her husband wanted her to be. From her clothes, makeup and shoes to where she shopped and whom she talked with; everything was dictated by her husband.

Her fear of losing him made her bend to his wishes however insulting, demeaning and traumatic it was to her. She justified her subservience believing it was worthwhile.

Fear also can turn a codependent partner into exhibiting frequent outbursts stemming from doubt and jealousy. Such extreme paranoia about a partner leaving is a clear indicator of codependency.

Emotional attachment

Amy and John had met at work and they had a whirlwind courtship that ended in marriage. Amy grew up in a dysfunctional family where her mother was the giver and her father the taker.

This had a lasting impact on her and she became so emotionally invested in the relationship with her husband that she did not want to do anything on her own. She began to rely on her husband not only for affection, but for emotional support and self-worth.

When you completely bury your own identity and take up a new one where you rely on your partner for your emotional and physical wellbeing, it turns into an unhealthy and codependent relationship.

When a relationship is healthy, both partners are equally invested in making it work. They feel comfortable doing things on their own like seeing their friends and having their own hobby. This does not happen in a codependent relationship.

Accepting toxic behavior

It is true that loving someone makes you turn a blind eye to their faults. But if you are codependent, you can easily miss the toxic behavior of your partner, when he manipulates you or makes unrealistic demands.

When you ignore these red flags, the situation will worsen with time and you will find it more difficult to come out of the relationship.

Being codependent does not mean that your love for your partner is not true. Instead of seeking love and mutual friendship and affection, you look to your partner for fulfilling some deep emotional need you have that cannot be satisfied on your won. This lays the foundation for a toxic relationship.

Remember that it is futile to keep on ignoring the faults of your partner or enabling them in their wrong doings. Your desire to be supportive can actually be a clear sign of your codependent behavior, one which you should get rid of at the earliest possible.

Knowing the signs and what they mean can help you identify them early on and take the necessary action. If you are putting too much effort on keeping your relationship going, take a break. Take some time to look closely at your relationship.

Is this what you want in your life?

When you are ready to go all in into a relationship, your partner should also be as committed to it as you are. You can be at this position, when you can spot the signs and seek proper support.

Chapter 2: Early signs of codependency you should not miss out on

Codependency is a dysfunctional relationship where one individual depends on the other for satisfying all their self-esteem and emotional needs. It enables the other person to continue with the addictive, irresponsible, and underachieving behavior.

- Are you exhausting yourself trying to meet the needs of your partner?
- Are you the only one making sacrifices in your relationship?

If your answer is yes to both the above questions, your relationship may be a codependent one.

There are some early signs that you can identify easily that point to a codependent relationship. Here are a few important signs you should look out for, if you suspect you are codependent. The signs are a warning and if you ignore them, they can worsen and move onto a point of no return.

However, they are completely reversible, if you catch them early on and take the necessary steps. So, let us look at these signs.

- **Shattered Self Esteem**

If you keep comparing yourself or feel that you are unworthy, these are signs that indicate you have low esteem. Many people who have low self-esteem issues actually act like they are super confident, when actually they feel inadequate or unlovable.

Deep in their consciousness they will keep their inadequacy well-hidden.

Perfectionism and guilt often go hand in hand with lowered self-esteem. You will not have the feeling of inadequacy, if everything is as you wish it to be, that is, perfect.

How low self-esteem influences a codependent relationship

Relationship issues are inevitable in codependency. And a key reason for this is lack of self-esteem. In fact, studies indicate that there is a definite link between relationship satisfaction and self-esteem.

The self-esteem level present during the initial diagnosis of codependency will determine the prognosis of the relationship. If your self-esteem was very low before the relationship, chances are slim for the success of the relationship.

This is because your personality and past experience will have a lasting effect on your self-esteem and on the relationship in particular.

The codependency factor

When your family is a dysfunctional one growing up, you are bound to have self-esteem issues. And since this happened during your growing years, you will not be able to avoid it.

With parents who have self-esteem issues, your needs and opinions will not be heard. Thus, you will not be exposed to good relationship traits like

- Observing healthy boundaries
- Being assertive
- Resolution of conflict
- Being cooperative

With parents who are preoccupied with their issues, indifferent, abusive, controlling, inconsistent, manipulative or interfering, the children's relationship traits become tainted. They feel abandoned and come to the conclusion that they are wanting or inadequate.

The feeling of toxic shame is internalized and they continue to feel angry, anxious or insecure. They are unable to trust others, hate who they are and do not feel safe with others. Thus, they grow up having low self-esteem and become codependent.

Codependency thus evolves due to the feelings of shame, insecurity and defective self-esteem they have. It becomes a style of attachment that is based on avoiding and anxiety. They do not develop close relationship, nor do they like being alone as both spurs on pain for them.

Anxiety in codependency

Feelings of anxiety causes a codependent to sacrifice his or her needs and try to accommodate and please at all times.

As a codependent you will be preoccupied with such dynamics due to the insecure feelings you have. This makes you highly sensitive to the needs of your partner and you will keep on worrying that your partner may not need your closeness.

You will perceive any action in a negative way and think of negative outcomes. You will try not to bring up an issue and keep a low profile. This results in compromising on real intimacy.

Feelings of jealousy are common in such a situation towards any person your partner speaks, texts or calls. Your repeated attempts of seeking reassurance will push your partner away.

Avoidance in codependency

Like anxiety, avoidance also causes a big rift in the relationship.

Distancing behavior like addiction, flirting, and unilateral decisions, ignoring the feelings or needs of the partner leads to dissatisfaction in the relationship. You are hypersensitive to the attempts made by your partner to limit or control you in any way.

Lack of communication

Proper communication is absent in dysfunctional families. Communication is vital in any relationship and more so in a codependent one. You need to speak honestly, clearly, assertively and concisely.

And most important of all, you should be capable of listening. This will ensure all the needs of a partner including the ability to define boundaries. With intimate relationship such skills are difficult to keep up. Because in intimate relationships, you need courage to assert your feelings.

You need to have self-acceptance, which will give you the power to honor your feelings so you can risk rejection and criticism while voicing your needs.

However, co-dependents lack the assertive nature and also deny their needs and wants due to the condition being developed in them from childhood.

The constant suppression of needs makes them depend on things like lying, blaming, asking questions, mindreading, caretaking and ignoring, controlling or avoiding their partner.

These can escalate any conflict; worsen to attacks, laying blame and subsequent withdrawal. The openness, happiness and closeness are totally avoided. In such situations, a partner may look for the closeness and happiness in another person thus your relationship enters shaky ground.

However shattered self-esteem need not be a hurdle to dealing with codependency. There are ways and means to reduce the shame and raise your self-esteem, which we will see in the last few chapters of this book.

- **Devoting Your Entire Actions To Pleasing Others**

Are you bending yourselves backwards to please others?

Being a people pleaser is not being kind or big hearted. It is not about compromising either. For people pleasers, the knowledge that they value a relationship and a compromise is needed for sustaining it, urges on the attitude. It soon becomes compulsive.

All of us begin our life with the need to be loved, accepted and safe. This is part of our makeup. But down the line, you start thinking that the best way is to set aside your feelings and wants. Gradually you start giving precedence to the feelings and needs of others.

While this can work for some time, it can further worsen issues along the way. You will not be able to say no and keep on taking up more work than you can manage.

You will start feeling resentful and land in a situation where you are judged, if you please and also when you do not. This causes problems in your relationship. While you try to please your partner, you will be left feeling unappreciated and with the feeling that your wants are ignored.

You will feel lost, bored and depressed. Feelings of hurt, resentment, conflict and anger rear their ugly heads. Staying alone may feel like you are being away from such happenings, but this can cause a rift between you and others. You are now at a point where you either chose sacrificing yourself or letting go of a relationship.

And at this level, you will find stopping not just difficult, but also downright terrifying. As you see people around you who are not people pleasers but are well liked you will be puzzled. You will start questioning yourself on how you landed in such a situation and your belief that people pleasing will make other people accept you.

The fear of disappointing others, rejection and guilt becomes overwhelming making you continue with the people pleasing attitude. You feel it is easier and hassle free to agree instead of objecting.

Just like self-esteem issues, this pleasing also develops as you grow up. You start with trying to please your parents to win their love and acceptance.

When you are a people pleaser, assertiveness, setting limits and stressing on meeting your needs may sound rude and demanding.

These feelings attract you to persons with opposing personality traits such as independent, powerful and certitude that you admire.

You will not be attracted to other similar people pleasers, as you think them as weak. In fact, subconsciously you dislike yourself for behaving so submissively.

Every time you put the needs of others over yours, you lose some self-respect and over a long time of continuing in this state, you will lose connection with your true self. This will leave you feeling empty without any passion or joy.

However, it is possible to reclaim your voice, power and passion. The self-reclamation journey is a worth one and you will be glad of learning and accomplishing it later in this book.

- **Lack Of Boundaries In Your Relationship**

In codependency there is weak or no personal boundaries at all. This is the reason for others disrespecting you. Furthermore, as a codependent you also disrespect or test boundaries of other people sorely.

Codependents are perceived as violated or disrespected victims. This is why support groups and therapies are aimed at encouraging them to learn setting boundaries with people so they avoid such violation.

However, not much is done about how you affect the boundaries of other people in order to be codependent. The absence of healthy boundaries is caused by dysfunctional relationships and emotional distress.

Why we need boundaries in a relationship

The very concept of boundaries is actually telling others what you can and cannot accept. The boundaries help people understand the way you want them to treat you.

By setting healthy boundaries, you can build genuine relationships. Boundaries are something respectful and loving you do to yourself as well as those around you. This is because the boundaries help you to communicate effectively.

People will know where they are at when it comes to relationships with you. You create adequate space for fun, intimacy and genuine connection in your life.

Without boundaries

When you ignore boundaries or do nothing when your boundaries are violated, it will seem as if you are alright with how you are treated or do not care at all. This happens in a codependent relationship often, as you do not want to express your needs and wants.

As a result, others ignore or disrespect your boundaries and so do you. This can be in the form of unwanted advice, demanding attention and time of others, over sharing or acting in a way that the other person has expressed concern about.

Respecting boundaries

Setting healthy boundaries needs cooperation from everyone involved. Without the boundaries, you will be subject to emotional distress.

So, how do you set this right?

- Learn about the value of boundaries
- Find out how to identify boundaries of others
- Learn to set boundaries
- Identify and respect boundaries of others

The problem with boundaries is that when others set them, we think it as an affront or insult.

This can trigger destructive argument and conflict due to the fact that you are ignorant of the value of boundaries in navigating relationships with others.

Yes, boundaries form a vital part of forming intimate and healthy relationships.

- **Communication gap**

Communication gap or poor communication is a major contributor to relationship conflicts. This is true in a codependent relationship too.

Kate shared a good relationship with her husband and both were friends before they married. They were open with each other and were able to talk about anything. But after marriage they lost the personal communication touch and became judgmental.

Kate's husband thought she was immature and stupid and told her so. His criticizing attitude made her stop sharing things with him. And her disapproval of his activities made him stop sharing any of his activities with her.

When you fail to listen and discourage your partner even when they act crazy, it causes a big rift between you. Maybe you could have explained the irrational behavior in a friendly way. Filtered expressions and half-hearted participation in conversations can weaken the bond between couples.

This is true in parent-children relationship too. When parents try to disapprove every act of their kids in a harsh way, kids begin hiding things. They start building a shell around themselves. Parents should make it such a way that their children are free to talk to them about anything without being judged.

When you communicate poorly, it can jeopardize the entire relationship. Communication breakdown symptoms include

- Arguing constantly
- Not listening to the other person
- Feeling like you are not talking about important matters
- Acting defensively

When there is communication gap, it will impact your self confidence and self-esteem. What you need for the relationship to move forward is to develop

- Mutual respect
- Openness
- Honesty
- Trust

In order to get away from a codependent relationship, you should develop relationships that are caring, supportive and productive. This happens when you develop good listening skills, which is a vital part of proper interpersonal communication.

You should be able to understand the perspective of the other person. Staying focused on the other person, compromising, finding mutually beneficial solutions and mutual caring are vital factors that help sustain a long lasting and healthy relationship.

- **Obsessive Behavior**

Obsessive behavior arises from persistent urges, obsessive thoughts and intrusive mental visions that lead to anxiety, disturbance and distress in a person. These can include

- Doubts regarding completion of a task as simple as turning off a stove
- Disturbing or unpleasant sexual images
- Fear of the other person acting in a way to harm you
- The need to keep personal effects, items or people in a particular order
- Afraid of being contaminated

The above thoughts lead to certain actions such as constant checking of locks, stoves, doors, switches etc., excessive cleaning, repeated counting, avoiding people or situations due to personal fears, uncontrollable thoughts of harming others or vice versa and obsessing about an object, person, substance or gambling.

Obsession will make you feel uncomfortable talking about the thoughts or feelings you experience. The thoughts will leave you feeling isolated, frightened, alone, and beyond help.

How obsessions impact a codependent relationship

Obsession dominates you and robs your will and the pleasure you take from life. You turn numb to events and people as your mind lingers on constant images or words.

You will have zero interest in what the other person speaks, and you will start talking about your obsessions ignoring its impact on the listener.

If the obsession is mild, you can use your work to distract yourselves. But when it is intense, all your actions and thoughts will be focused on the obsession. The behavior will not be under your conscious control and does not listen to reasoning.

Thus, obsessive behavior can take control of your mind. You will focus on thoughts that feed incessant fantasy, worry and you keep searching for answers. This takes over your entire life making you lose your sleep and time that you could have spent productively and enjoyably.

Obsessions lead to compulsive behavior like constantly checking weight, the locks on doors, email, text messages and more. You start losing touch with your feelings and reasoning ability. Such obsessions are caused by fear.

Addiction and obsession

In codependents who are addicts, the focus is on the objection of addiction such as alcohol, food, sex and more. The behavior and thinking are concentrated on the addiction, while the true self is shrouded in shame.

The feeling of shame and preoccupation of how others perceive us causes anxiety and obsessions related to how people consider your past, present and even future actions.

Shame spurs feelings of doubt, insecurity, guilt and indecision. Normally guilt can become obsession leading to self-shaming, but it can be treated by taking corrective action. However, shame continues in a codependent relationship, as here it is not your actions that you find fault with but your own self.

Relationship suffers due to your obsession

A codependent usually obsesses about people he or she loves and cares about including the issues faced.

You might worry about the alcoholic addiction of your partner not understanding that you are preoccupied with the person in the same way as the person is focused on the addiction.

Obsessive behavior can spur you to control others in ways such as

- Stalking someone
- Going through the other person's diary, texts, or emails
- Hiding keys

All the above action causes further conflict and havoc in the relationship. While it is perfectly normal in a budding relationship to focus on what your partner is doing, in codependents it does not end there.

When you are not obsessing about the relationship, you focus on the whereabouts of your partner or stir up jealousy that damages the relationship.

The obsession can also be about fantasies you dream of like power, sex or romance that you want to be better in the relationship.

When there is a huge gap between what you dream of and the reality, it will affect your behavior.

Why obsessive behavior occurs in codependency?

Obsession is triggered when you are unable to tolerate the painful emotions. Obsessive behavior occurs as a means to protect yourself from the painful feelings.

You create it as a defense to your underlying emotions of shame, fear, emptiness, anger, grief or loneliness.

Fear of being rejected by your partner, or losing the partner to addiction can also turn into obsessive behavior.

While in some cases the obsessive behavior may be genuine, like when you are afraid your partner may get sick due to overdose or get arrested or even kill someone while drunk.

Or, it can be in the form of obsessing over trivial things to avoid facing a much bigger issue.

If you are perfectionist, you may obsess about a flaw in your appearance, instead of acknowledging your inferiority complex, which is the real issue here.

How can this obsessive behavior be tackled?

Just as obsession is the way you behave to avoid your deepest feelings of insecurity, by reacquainting with those feelings you can help dissolve the obsessive behavior.

If your obsessive behavior prevents you from taking proactive action, you can seek support to face your fears.

Meditation, evocative music, spending time with nature, embracing spirituality, improving your social skills, focusing on creative pastime or simply focusing on doing what makes you happy you can deal with the obsessive behavior.

- **Denial**

Denial in codependency is the need to avoid distressing, emotional or discomfort causing thoughts spurred by others and for your own survival.

Denial is a type of coping mechanism that develops from childhood and can also be termed as defense mechanism. It helps you avoid stress, depression and anxiety when faced with bad things or uncomfortable issues.

As you grow, you hone these denial patterns to tackle any issue you face in life, even if they do not work.

While denial is a practical behavior pattern that helps you face an emotionally distress causing situation, it can turn into dangerous and harmful pattern. It can allow you to stay in an emotionally damaging relationship or one that is physically abusive.

Denial develops when you try to avoid feelings of shame, loss, fear, conflict or neglect in the family. It is your way to pretend that dysfunction is not present or does not affect you emotionally.

Common signs of denial include

- Making yourself believe that something you have experienced is not affecting you or minimizing a hurtful, abusive or negative interaction
- Making excuses for your partner's bad behavior
- Believing that your behavior pattern will change in spite of repeated proof that it will not happen any time in the future
- Instead of focusing on what is happening, you keep thinking about what could have been and not
- Rationalizing your behavior and that of your partner
- Ignoring or reducing the pain inflicted on you
- Accepting broken promises and empty apologies

While some codependents act needy, there are others who act self-sufficient pretending that they do not need help. They will not reach out and find it difficult to receive help.

They deny their vulnerability and their need for intimacy and love. Their fear of being rejected is the main reason for refusing their help.

Seeking Help

Denial is part of the defense mechanism that codependents develop. Denial in codependency is therefore characterized by the need for feeling needed, shattered self-esteem, inadequacy and self-love.

One important result of treating the denial behavior is highlighting all existing behaviors connected to codependency. Once the codependent person is aware of the denial, he or she can seek support and help in changing the behavior pattern.

Proper therapy, coaching and support can help identify the pattern and help deal with it in a healthy, effective and positive way.

Recognition of individuality and allowing blossoming of self-love can happen, when the appropriate therapy is provided.

- **Feelings Of Despair, Fear, Hopelessness, Guilt, And Depression**

As you now know, codependency is made of several distinct traits or characteristics. These include behavioral patterns like denial, obsession and emotional traits like despair, guilt, fear, depression and hopelessness.

It is not the number of traits you have that decides you are codependent, but on how they impact your emotional and physical health.

Feelings of despair are natural in codependency because of the following reasons

- Feelings of shame and inferiority that fester for a long time
- Falling into unsuccessful relationships
- Constant issues that you cannot come out of
- Being beholden to an unhealthy relationship
- Feeling hopeless due to continuing feelings of stress, insecurity and lack of peace
- Not having your needs met
- Feeling lonely
- Feelings of abandonment
- Losing faith in the possibility of a better and improved future

Progressing to Depression

Despair and hopelessness of your situation can lead to feeling listless and numb. You may feel as if you are drained of life. You start losing interest in activities that you loved to do.

You will be engulfed by sadness and the need to cry without feeling any relief. Depression can result due to suppression of your feelings of anger and despair. The negative attitude you develop due to shame also triggers depression.

While mild depression is natural in codependent relationship, it is often masked or suppressed by the busy routine, caretaker responsibilities, excitement of sex and romance, melodrama in relationship and other such things.

Deep depression occurs when you are not able to bounce back after an emotional setback. Thus, instead of having feelings of despair and sadness you can enter into a depressive episode.

Unlike the typical feelings of anxiety and despair that you normally feel, depression can be debilitating. It can disrupt your life and affect your ability to complete even the most mundane work.

You will withdraw from activities, your cognitive and motor functions will slow, and there will be changes in your sleeping habits. You will have irrational feelings of shame or guilt and have difficulty in focusing on making decisions.

The above symptoms cause high level of distress. You will experience impairment in important functional areas including occupational, social and educational. Your mood will be down persistently and improve when you feel better for a long period. However, if left untreated, the depression can return and stay for longer span.

Feeling inadequate

While stress is an important cause for depression, the actual cause in a codependent relationship is the inadequacy you feel.

Your attempts to compensate for the inadequacy, your sacrificial self-care or feeling of being unworthy of love all trigger the depression. You fail to recognize that the root cause of the depression and despair is due to the codependency and your childhood experiences.

Due to the addiction to substances, people or obsessive behavior, codependents lose contact with their true inner self. This robs them of their vitality leading to depression.

Denial also causes depression. The denial of needs, feelings, problems, abuse and need to control things can add to hopelessness about the situation they are in. When the codependency remains untreated, over time it can worsen the hopelessness and despair you feel.

The goal of treatment in such conditions is encouraging development of coping skills, healing the root cause, changing feelings of shame, unlovability, and inadequacy.

Chapter 3: Difference between a Normal and Codependent Relationship

In a normal relationship, it is natural for the individuals involved to depend on one another. However, a codependent relationship is different. It is not like the dependency you see in a healthy relationship.

What does a healthy relationship look like?

We are social beings and have been living in groups relying on one another for our survival, food and shelter. It is therefore not wrong to need others and rely on them when you need help. This type of healthy dependency is termed as interdependency.

The normal dependent relationship is a healthy one where there is mutual sharing of support, help and encouragement.

But in a codependent relationship, there is gross imbalance. One person keeps sacrificing for the other without receiving anything in return.

This is a toxic relationship that results in burnout, dissatisfaction and resentment.

In a healthy interdependent relationship, there is enhanced self-esteem, mutual respect, confidence, master and emotional security.

The help, support and encouragement you get from your partner will help you feel safe and confident in tackling any issues you face. It will allow you to overcome any fear and help you grow as an individual.

Thus, there is a perfect balance of independence and dependence. The healthy interdependence does not prevent you from forging ahead and provides you the prop you need for improving yourself.

In an interdependent relationship, the persons involved will feel competent and express their need. They accept help from others but do not depend on them to improve their self-esteem.

In a codependent relationship, the codependent person is not aware of who he or she is, what they want and how to live as a separate identity.

In short, in a normal and healthy interdependent relationship your identity is not compromised. You can receive and give help while retaining your autonomy and individuality.

Why codependency is unhealthy?

In a codependent relationship, there is over dependence of one person on another. You feel your identity is fully intermeshed with that of your partner.

Your focus is to such a magnitude that your goals, interests and needs are ignored or suppressed.

While you may hold a job and are capable of paying bills and taking care of your children, you have this unhealthy desire to feel needed. This desire makes you dependent so you can stay feeling lovable and worthy.

Self-worth for a codependent is based on fixing, helping and rescuing others. This causes an imbalance in the relationship.

Only when both individuals involved accept their roles of giver and taker can the codependent relationship work.

However, it is not at all healthy to sacrifice your needs to feel valued and accepted. This is because the unworthy and flawed feeling creates toxic dependency where you always look to others to validate your beliefs, interests and your existence.

The need or craving to be wanted can leave you trapped in an unhappy, unfulfilling and abusive relationship. Without the caregiver role, you will feel unloved and purposeless.

Enabling is different from helping

In a healthy interdependent relationship, there is mutual support and help where each person has room to grow.

Codependent relationship on the other hand has one person as enabler, doing or rescuing things for the other instead of helping the partner to do things on their own.

The craving for being needed is very powerful and it unconsciously makes you an enabler. The enabled partner will be dependent and dysfunctional as if they are healthy, sober or employed, you will lose your purpose of taking care of them. Without the purpose you will feel unworthy.

This triggers you into acting in such a way that you persistently nag, give unnecessary advice and enable. Helping and enabling differ as helping encourages you to become confident and self-sufficient.

Codependency affects growth

Unlike an interdependent relationship where the people involved are encouraged to grow in all aspects including professional, emotional, spiritual and social, codependent relationship is abusive and unhealthy.

This is because the relationship concentrates on maintaining an imbalance where the giver can go on giving and gain self-esteem by enabling, while the taker has his financial, emotional and physical needs met.

Codependent persons will find it very difficult to function independently due to their self-worth issues and their consistent need to rely on others.

While relationship is vital to your existence adding joy and satisfaction to your life, it cannot fix the underlying wounds in you that you carry into a relationship.

You replay the dysfunctional relationship dynamics and worsen the relationship until the root cause is healed.

Understanding codependency and interdependency

It is difficult to recognize the difference between interdependent and codependent relationship, if you have never been exposed to a normal and healthy relationship.

Here is a table from Webster University on differences between the two relationships. The table will help you clear any doubts you have regarding the nature of your relationship or how a normal and healthy one can look like.

Codependent	Interdependent
Compelled, driven, intense, compulsive, and possessive. Compulsive need to keep partner so tied to the other that every thought, word, and action is guarded.	**Freedom of choice individuality, promoting growth. Partner acts in the other's best interest and gives them room and encouragement to grow and express their own individuality**
Enmeshed identities, feeling threatened by differences Suffocating closeness and attitude of "You have to be just like me."	**Separate identities, good self-esteem, values differences Self-esteem comes from within, not from the other person; partners value the differences of the other.**
Attributes strength of relationship, the other person or control over the other person. I can't live with your mentality or dictator/servant roles.	**Attributes strength to two separate entities working together to achieve a mutual goal. Strength comes from within not through the other person.**
Intense ups and downs. Cycle of behavior from good to violent; assumes the roles of victim, victimizer, and rescuer at certain intervals of the cycle.	**Consistency and predictability. Maintains consistent attitude of respect; partner knows what to expect in any situation and can trust the others commitment.**

Narrow support system one or both partners crowd out other relationships or isolate themselves or their partner from other people, including family.	**Broad support system. Both partners include outside activities to bring a healthy balance and growth to their relationship.**
Stock-market syndrome or people pleasers. One partner reacts to the mood of the other. If he is having a bad day, you have a bad day. If he is happy you are happy.	**Stable self-esteem. You sympathize care for the other person, but you do not take on their hurt or problems as your own.**
Refusal to deal with the past, denying and repeating problems. Repeats dysfunctional behavior of parents, but denies there are any problems.	**Open to periodic evaluation and opportunities for change. Evaluates the relationship and is open to healthy change and growth.**
Need to control or be controlled: manipulative; self-centered. "I want what I want when I want it "or " you do exactly what I say or else" attitude; often very critical and verbally abusive.	**Mutual submission. Surrendering power for the other person's own good; relinquishing your rights and not keeping score**
Dishonesty and refusal to admit wrong. Won't admit faults; demands all family members to keep quiet about life at home; rationalizes and lies to cover up bad behavior.	**Honest and characterized by integrity. Admits and makes amends for wrong behavior; motives are not self-centered; speaks directly and honestly; can be trusted.**

Although the differences between the two relationships are clear, you may still not be able to recognize you are in a codependent relationship that easily.

You have to put in real effort to reflect on your situation and be honest with your feelings. Even if you become aware of the relationship, refraining from such behavior is a difficult task one that needs perseverance and strong will to break the chain and get help to heal and resume a normal and healthy relationship.

PART III: The Proactive Phase

Now that you know what a codependent relationship is and how it is different from a healthy and interdependent one, it is time to do something about it. Granted it is not easy to recognize much less accept that you are codependent.

The fear of the unknown and fear of failure can keep you from taking the positive step forward. You have to overcome the strong beliefs you have formed and your fears that hold you from trying.

You may be afraid to be free from your present life, which you consider as your safe haven, regardless of how you have lost your own identity.

Don't be a worrier

Avoid dreaming of multiple scenarios on what will happen, if you break up from the relationship. Many people tend to do this to avoid possible failures and to find out the quickest way out of a terrible situation.

However, this can be taken to the extreme causing you to stop contemplating the change. You will be paralyzed and terrified of the outcomes you are imagining.

One way to deal with such a behavior is to make strong decisions and stop wasting your effort on worrying about things that are yet to occur. Too much worrying can be a big hurdle to make the changes you want.

Remember the good times

To make change possible, you have to quit worrying and set aside some time to go over the good times in your life when change had worked out well for you.

When you look back, the bad decisions are the first things that you can visualize. But when you take some time, you can recognize the times in your life when you had successfully embraced change.

Thinking about such changes, which ended up good for you in spite of the highs and lows will be a big encouragement for you.

When I took up my job, I had to juggle looking after my kids both in their preschool stage, and without help from my husband, because he did not like me working.

The thought that I was able to bring up my kids and still work reminded me that if I set my mind to it, I could certainly get out of the relationship.

Grab opportunity with both hands

Even if you do decide that change is good for you, you can sometimes become stuck on how to go about it.

You have to be broad minded and look at the opportunities before you. Getting rid of codependency is not an easy task.

But there are several ways to approach your issues, treat them and heal your mind and body. To see them, you have to first be open to embracing the change. Your full effort is needed to come out of your self-imposed captivity.

Get rid of toxic routines

Having a routine is good as it makes you disciplined and reduces decision stress and in general makes your daily work easier.

However, this will not help when you want to make changes in your life. Your routine can play spoil sport and prevent you from taking a new direction.

To untangle yourself from the mess of codependent relationship, you have to get into a proactive mode.

Start by making minor changes to your daily routine like the food you eat, the route you take to your work etc. Such minor changes will give you a fresh perspective and help you gear up for the bigger move. You will gain more confidence and take the necessary steps.

Chapter 1: Is it possible to be free of a codependent relationship?

When you finally recognize and accept that you are in a codependent relationship, it is just the beginning of your journey to get rid of the behavior.

Once you get over the shock of being a victim to codependent behavior pattern, you may wonder whether it is really possible to be free of it?

The constant emotional fluctuation between fear of abandonment and wanting to be loved can turn into a frustrating push and pull that leaves you and your partner exhausted.

When you realize your predicament, you need to rethink your position in the relationship. The anxieties and fears that controlled your behavior will prevent you from having a meaningful relationship.

The deeply ingrained codependent patterns are difficult to erase overnight. Just as recovery from addiction takes time, patience and support, codependency too needs a careful approach.

Controlling your urges

The subconscious mind keeps pulling you towards satisfying your selfish desires, letting you succumb to the craving for your codependent behavior. And this will continue on, if you keep listening to your subconscious mind.

However, this can be stopped when you heed to your rational mind and control your cravings. Slowly and gradually you can chip away at these negative urges and get to the point where you do not feel their presence.

Breaking the pattern

The early childhood experiences that nurture the codependent behavior leave behind an unshakeable belief that you are not safe. The codependent behavior is thus directly linked to your survival instinct making it difficult to get rid of.

Early on codependents learn to control their feelings and emotions as they are afraid of revealing them for fear of being abused or abandoned.

Or, they turn manipulative and demanding resulting in a havoc filled emotional push and pull between rejection fear and craving to feel recognized.

While you take the necessary and firm steps towards breaking free, you will find that the codependency thoughts keep surfacing up at odd moments in your day.

You are dragged back to the doubtful and fear inducing thoughts that threaten to pull you down. This is why codependents are in an emotionally weak state after they split up.

Since your codependent behavior has been with you for a long time, you tend to automatically go into the negative pattern of monitoring the emotions of others, predicting their actions and changing your actions and thoughts in an effort to make you feel you belong. This pattern turns into destructive and unhealthy behavior when you become an adult.

But all is not lost. There is still hope and you can shut down the manipulative behavior and get rid of the need to have the approval of those around you. To do this, you need to love yourself first and accept who you are.

Not heeding to your codependent thoughts will interrupt the pattern and will make you feel free of the regret, toxic shame and guilt that arise due to such thoughts.

The self-inflicted pain which you think you deserve due to the toxic shame should and can be stopped.

Interrupt your toxic thoughts and feelings with positive affirmations and associations. This will help you get rid of the toxic web of feelings and reactions.

The change can take some time to happen. Until then hold on for you deserve your happy and fulfilling life just as every other person on this earth.

Understand your codependent state

The first step towards freedom and healing is to understand how your happiness, belief in yourself and your moods are defined by your partner.

Does your partner's depressed mood make you moody?

Do you use dishonest methods to avoid confrontation for fear of abandonment?

Or, do you feel the need to control and keep demanding things from your partner?

Recognizing such patterns will help in deciding the solution for your predicament.

You can start healing and move past it only when you know who you are and where you are at.

Stop the blame game

Avoid placing the blame on your partner for your codependent state. The sad truth about codependency is that there is not just a single person who is responsible for the derailing of a relationship.

From dysfunctional family relationships and past disappointments to resentments and present issues you have numerous factors that impact on the way you behave.

The only way to deal with this is to remove yourself from the conflicting emotions.

Meditation and taking an objective view of your relationship can help you identify patterns and detach yourself from the expectations you have built.

Start setting boundaries

Instead of blurring the lines between you and your partner, set boundaries and improve your self-esteem. This can be done by

- Understanding your core values such as the time and effort you spend on your work, family, passion, religion and culture. The time you spend on such aspects and help you define what is vital for you. This will keep your needs in focus and they will not be eclipsed by the needs of your partner.
- Instead of attempting to change those around you, take responsibility and make the changes in you. Focus on self-improvement.
- Spend time daily to reflect on the events of the day so you feel connected to your inner self always.

When you set firm boundaries, you will not be afraid of saying no. You will be able to distance yourself from situations and relationships that are unhealthy.

Remember that the key purpose of relationships is to complement your life and not take up your whole life.

Breaking from codependent pattern will help you focus on yourself and take the steps necessary for self-growth.

Stop putting yourself down and turn your negative thoughts to positive ones. It is up to you to take the all important first step of understanding your situation and that you need help. The rest of it will happen much easier than you think.

Chapter 2: 7 steps you should consider for a healthy relationship

Realizing you are in a codependent relationship can be depressing and wreak havoc with your emotions, thoughts and actions.

But do not despair. There is always a way out of any situation. You have to just know where to find it. When you do, you can make the effort needed to step into a healthy relationship.

When you find that the spiteful actions, toxic behavior and constant arguing is exhausting you beyond limits, it's time to look for the steps that will get you out of the rut you are in.

Here are 7 important steps that will ensure you are heading in the right direction.

1. Explore

Learn more about what is codependency and how to differentiate it from a healthy interpersonal relationship. Read self-help books which help you find yourself.

Acknowledge your codependent state. Identify and isolate the actions and thoughts that keep you codependent. Try making the necessary positive behavioral modification that will help you in building a healthy relationship

2. Recognize patterns

Your previous relationships and experiences have led to the emotional dependent state you are in. These cause you to exhibit codependent behavior.

To be free of the emotional tangles, you have to recognize where the existing behavior pattern stemmed from.

When you find out the root cause of your behavior, you will be able to assess your situation in a better way. You can then know what to do to change your emotional state and become independent.

3. Self-care is the right step forward

You start depending on your partner for emotional support, when you fail to know how to take care of yourself emotionally.

Depending on others gives you a feeling of being connected. It satisfies your emotional needs but disregards your capability of self-validation.

You have to stand up for yourself to stop this emotional dependency.

Find out what you are expecting in your partner or relative that makes you emotionally dependent.

Can you satisfy those needs without relying on the other person?

4. Welcome solitude

Some alone time is vital for each one of us, irrespective of how healthy or unhealthy our relationship with others is. Spending time alone helps you to reflect on your day, reactions with others, your actions and other things.

Even spending some time on a solo activity that you enjoy can give you the breather you need. And it is not selfish to spend some time alone.

The time alone will help you reconnect with yourself. It will help you relearn about independence. You can find your space where you can be yourself without fear of abandonment, retribution or rejection.

Taking up hobbies you like and those that can be enjoyed on your own is a good step in this direction. It can be painting, yoga or learning to play a musical instrument, pottery classes or anything that attracts your attention or those that you have wanted to do for a long time.

Carve some alone time out of your busy routine. Do solo activities. Reach out to peace, comfort and joy all by yourself. When you grasp on how to be yourself, your emotional independence will not be far behind.

5. Find out your strengths

Write down a list of things you are good at regardless of how trivial they may be. Finding about your strengths gives you confidence and helps you become independent emotionally. This is because you will realize that you have a lot to give whatever relationship you are in.

Try to build on your strengths and make them bigger. Focus on your positive point's one at a time. Keep reminding yourself how good you are at it.

When you know about your strong points, you will not be looking to others to corroborate it and make you feel good.

You will start feeling good all on your own. This boosts your confidence and helps you think, act and live independently.

6. Observe people around you

Take a close look at the people you are in a relationship with. Find out what you like and admire about these people.

Now look at yourself and find if you have those traits in you. If you are with people you admire, they would not be with you, if you don't have similar traits.

A person does not deliberately seek out a negative and needy person. If you are such a person, you will attract similar people in your life. To build a loving and healthy relationship, you should learn to be emotionally responsible.

It is easy to find faults in your partner, but very difficult to see where you are at in a dysfunctional relationship.

If self-abandonment and self-care is lacking in you, so will it be in your partner. Both of you will be emotionally affected.

Jane complains of Michael criticizing her at every turn. Jane is likely blaming herself and surrendering to Michael in order to wield control over getting his approval. Thus, both end up being controlling. However, Jane is just aware of her husband's controlling nature.

To attract a healthy relationship, you need to first heal your feelings of insecurity and shame. You have to stop abandoning yourself and learn to love yourself.

Take responsibility for your feelings instead of avoiding them or hoisting the responsibility on another person.

Value yourself. Learn to take responsibility for your feelings. This will keep you away from emotionally needy people. You will avoid individuals who are judging, withdrawn or see themselves as victims.

Neutralize negative thoughts

When you are emotionally dependent and crave validation, avoid letting negative emotions and thoughts to discourage you from moving forward.

Instead of pushing out the negative thoughts, you can counter them with an equally strong positive affirmation. This will be easier to accomplish than getting rid of negative emotions.

Make sure the positive thoughts you hold on to are realistic. This is because many a time, the positive affirmations can become unrealistic and make you avoid them altogether.

When negative thoughts hold you captive, bring in the compassionate positive emotions. Make them go together so one does not override the other.

Eventually the negative emotions will take a hike as you gain confidence and take sure and stronger steps forward.

Be confident and self-assured

One key reason for codependence is the absence of self-confidence. You will not have the self-assurance needed to know your value.

The codependent relationship will make you seek your self-worth from what you do and not from who you are. You will find it difficult to voice your needs.

You will feel happy depending on others and feel satisfied only when your partner is happy. Your lack of trust in your capability will make you took to others for solution to your issues.

When you have strong self-value, you will not allow others to control your self-esteem. No one but you can decide your worth.

And remember that you can truly love others only when you love yourself. And while people may enter your life and leave it at any point in time, the only one who stays with you forever is your own self.

When you neglect to love yourself and value yourself, your relationships suffer and turn destructive.

A significant portion of recovery is identifying a new supportive connection. While some turn to religion there are others who join support groups, mediations, inspirational videos and more to destress themselves and connect with their body and mind.

Depending on your partner to complete you is a very painful and destructive part of codependency. Recovery entails your willingness to confront your dependent behavior and your steps towards becoming self-reliant.

When you are free of the tangled web of codependency, you will find that the relationships you build take on the appropriate place, which is behind the relationship you have nurtured with yourself.

In the end, your change for the better lies solely in your hands.

While support groups, counselors and other programs can help you identify and point you to the steps you can take to change your behavior, you have to take the conscious decision of looking after yourself.

This is the healthiest and smartest thing you that you are capable of that can spare you from the clutches of a codependent relationship.

When you fail to take care of yourself, the responsibility falls on others, which will again land you in a codependent relationship. When you persevere and take the necessary steps to come out of a toxic codependent relationship, you can start anew.

You may wonder whether there is chance of a codependent relationship being salvaged. This is possible only when the individuals involved work together to make shift the relationship to an interdependent one.

In an interdependent relationship, both partners provide something to make the relationship work and both benefit from it. If this is possible, then the chances of salvaging a codependent relationship are high.

Chapter 3: Embark on a journey of self-realization

Self-discovery is a goal that everyone should achieve. Many people live their life without showing their true self. There are others who turn into what others expect them to be.

Codependents belong to the latter group. Knowing yourself is an important aspect that impacts you in every stage of your life. Self-discovery helps you identify your objective in life and boosts your potential.

If you fail to embark on self-realization journey, you will cheat yourself of the opportunity to understand yourself and what you want in your life.

When you start out, it is natural to feel nervousness and anxiety. You may even be afraid of how the journey may affect your deeper feelings.

Fear not, for all hidden emotions will definitely benefit from your self-realization. The exposure will help you deal effectively with all your fears, doubts and negativity and clear them.

And when you come across positive things such as skills, courage and strength, use them to achieve your goals. In short, prepare yourself to accept what you find and forge ahead.

When you courageously face your traits that are revealed by your realization journey, you can grow stronger.

But remember that you need to accept your codependent state and the limitations it brings. This will help you work out the weaker traits and emerge a better individual. You can start enjoying your stronger points and savor them every day.

- **Change is inevitable**

Change is the only constant thing in our world. This is a simple but very profound fact. It brings to mind Einstein's insanity definition, which is repeatedly doing a thing expecting a different outcome every time.

Codependency cycle can be broken only when you start establishing a loving relationship with yourself and start nurturing it. Failing to do this will land you in a chain of codependent and unhealthy relationships.

Change symbolizes the life you lead from birth. Whether it is emotional, physical, career related or your relationships, change is required for your betterment.

In order to survive, you have to accept change and not resist it. Resistance will only lead to more pain.

Don't resist change

Getting out of your comfort zone to which you have become accustomed to is really difficult. There are many reasons why people resist change such as

- Being very comfortable with your present situation
- Fear of failing
- Fear of uncertainty when you enter a new dimension

Being trapped in may not be/ may be

Let me show you an example. Elizabeth had just broken up with her boyfriend and she meets a person at work that she is interested in. Her earlier relationship had left her sad, depressed and lacking, which makes her afraid to commit herself to the new one.

She is bombarded by several hurdles that prevent her from making the leap. Her doubts and insecurities keep her trapped in a miserable space.

Uncertainty

Fear of making the wrong direction and landing back in the same position as before with even worse emotional scars

Not ready to face the change and adjust to it

Many times, people reject an opportunity forgetting that change is good and rejuvenating. Change helps you explore your hidden talents and skills.

Welcome change wholeheartedly

Don't be rigid in your stand. Instead encourage and welcome changes in your life. This will open you up to new opportunities and create the right atmosphere for a healthy relationship.

To survive and grow, you need to go with the flow. Trees that can bend during a storm survive while the erect or rigid ones get uprooted.

Although changing those around you is not possible, you can make changes in your life so you are accepted. Change your perspective and embrace it.

What doesn't kill you makes you stronger

You cannot always control things around you. And it is not possible to avoid the changes that happen around you.

But you can always learn to adjust to the changes.

What you will find difficult is, if your partner is not open to the change. I have experienced this in my life. My husband was so narcissistic that he was not able to accept the change when he had all he wanted through my codependent behavior.

Understand what your role is in the relationship. This will help you to change your contribution in the relationship dynamic. This will challenge your partner to make changes in the way they relate with you.

And remember that the inflated superiority and selfishness they feel is actually a battered self esteem and inadequacy. By focusing on my self-worth and self-confidence, I was able to hold my own and break away from the toxic relationship.

A narcissist should take up transcendent objectives and invest in the care of others. In contrast to a codependent person, what they need to do is practice their focus on others instead of themselves.

So, instead of complaining or being angry about things not going your way, be patient.

You will adapt to the changes when you persevere and pray to god asking for courage and wisdom to face the changes. As the saying goes, what doesn't kill you makes your stronger. As you accept the change, it will make you stronger and wiser.

Changes are vital to live and savor your life. To move forward in life, you have to accept change.

• Controlling never helps

Power is part of any relationship. It helps you wield control, have choices and enables you to influence your environment.

And using your power to satisfy your needs and wants is an instinctive and healthy habit. Being empowered helps you deal with your emotions effectively.

You will be confident of having a say in the outcomes in your life. Instead of just reacting to circumstances, you can act in an appropriate way.

Feeling powerless and weak

While empowerment is a good thing, not many of us feel it. Particularly when you are in a codependent relationship, you feel powerless and feel that you are controlled by outside forces.

And many people cede control voluntarily feeling uncomfortable using their own power or believe that doing so will makes others reject them.

So, you just react and focus on the needs and wants of your partner. Making decisions is difficult and so is taking action on your own. You feel mean about expressing your own emotions and feelings.

The reasons for this feeling of powerlessness are multiple. These include

- Constant external focus
- Being dependent on your partner
- Absence of assertiveness and deferring to decisions of others
- Feeling uncomfortable with power and believing that it harms your relationship
- Abandonment and rejection fears
- Denying your wants, feelings and needs
- Constant need for approval
- Harboring unreasonable expectations
- Not taking responsibility for your feelings and actions

Power and relationships

Imbalance of power in relationships is a common occurrence and particularly in a codependent one. When you fail to accept your power and avoid expressing yourself due to one or more of the above-mentioned reasons, you are letting others fill the void.

This is why it is common to see one of the partners in a codependent relationship being an abuser, narcissist or an addict and thus rides rough shod over the other.

The submissive partner generally uses indirect ways like withholding to exert his or her influence. When this happens for a long time, it can cause depression and other symptoms including physical symptoms.

In healthy relationships, there is always a struggle for supremacy in different aspects including who does the chores, handling finances and spending free time. To avoid the struggle from escalating to unmanageable proportions, couples generally divide up the domains ceding control to each other in specific areas.

Conventionally, while the man of the house looked after finances and earning, the woman's role was to take care of the home and kids. This is a natural progression in several families even in the current scenario where women have much better earning power.

But in recent years there is a shift in the dynamics with men participating more in parenting, childcare and other chores. Having a career provides women the confidence and knowledge that they can function independently. This gives them power.

Many individuals start resenting and feel frustrated when they do not share the work equally and rue over the imbalance power and unfairness. This occurs when your partner ignores your needs and feelings.

When your inputs are not heeded, you start feel that you are not important and get a powerless and disrespected feeling.

Power balance

Autonomy and self-worth are necessary, if you want your need for respect and feelings being reciprocated.

Unlike a healthy relationship where both partners contribute towards the relationship and take responsibility, a codependent relationship is an unbalanced and dysfunctional one.

The decisions are mutual and both feel valued and safe. Intimacy in relationships and the relationships as such need boundaries.

Without boundaries you cannot risk being honest about your feelings. You will feel threatened. Boundaries ensure you are happy and have mutual respect.

In codependency, power is perceived in a dysfunctional manner. When you grow in a dysfunctional family where power is used for exerting control you are subject to constant criticism or your feelings are totally ignored.

In such a situation, you grow up believing that love and power cannot exist together. You are afraid of your own power and use indirect means to meet your needs that is by people pleasing attitude or by accommodating others.

Or, in some families, children start exerting power to get what they need. Such developmental influences present with several issues when you are in a relationship.

Resentment and fear are dominant and it makes your partner resort to passive aggressive behavior or withdraw from you.

With controlling parents, children can rebel and act willfully or stubborn, or try to behave authoritatively. These can become huge hurdles in meeting your needs.

You end up being unsure of how to be assertive and make decisions even for yourself. Relinquishing control to your partner is the only way for you. Codependents do not have the self-esteem and autonomy, but assertiveness and self-esteem can be developed.

Reclaiming power

To reclaim power, you need to understand the different between control and power. When you take responsibility for your own happiness, it empowers you. Instead you try to focus on external factors or people to be happy. This leads to controlling behavior. So, what you need to do is

- Live consciously
- Take sole responsibility for yourself and the choices you make in life
- Build self esteem
- State your needs and desires clearly and directly

When you express your feelings and desires honestly you can set boundaries, refuse when you are not willing to accede, and have mutual respect. You will also allow your partner to act in a similar manner.

Autonomy is vital for building self-esteem and it helps you to learn to survive on your own. You will not look to others for approval and there is less reactive emotions and more interactions. You will start sharing your needs and feelings.

Finding solutions for your issues will be easier and so will be negotiating without the blame game or being defensive. When you assert your power it nurtures love, intimacy and makes you feel safe.

- **Obsessive behavior is not healthy**

Codependents are constantly worrying about those around them or their relationship. This stems from their dependent state, their anxieties and fears. There is also preoccupation about any mistakes they made or they think they might do.

In some cases, you start dreaming about how you would like to be loved to avoid the painful state you are in at present. This is also part of denial about your behavior.

I was under the wrong impression that obsession and love were the same. I was willing to do everything that my husband wanted in the naïve belief that it would make me happy.

Breathing space

But now I know that true love needs the contribution of both partners. Each partner has to have individual identity.

Both should spend some time apart doing things on their own like working on personal projects, meeting friends or just some alone time.

This allows you to connect effectively without feeling suffocated when you with each other. Instead of encroaching each other's space, the breathing room affords to give you a good perspective of the relationship.

Take the bull by its horns

Obsessive behavior needs to be stopped before it wreaks havoc with your relationship, emotions and health.

To stop the behavior, you have to first recognize the obsessive thoughts. Since the obsessive pattern becomes a well-established habit, it will become an unconscious act on your part.

However, try to be conscious of your thoughts and stop your thoughts when you find you are obsessing over something.

Another way to deal with obsession is writing down the thoughts. This will help you recognize what triggers such thoughts and your reaction to the thoughts.

Identify the underlying reason for such thoughts to get a clear perspective. If you are worrying about your partner not texting you or replying to your texts, look for the root cause. Worrying about not receiving a text can actually be your anxiety of your partner not loving you as you do.

Accept the obsessive thoughts instead of suppressing or ignoring them, which will make them bigger than they seem. When you accept instead of avoiding or controlling your thoughts, you will be able to look at them objectively.

To do this, you have to be focused on your present and know the extent of your control. Worrying about what may happen in the future will not prevent it. Acceptance will help to reign in your thoughts and break away from the pattern.

- **Enjoy every breathing moment**

To truly be free of your codependent state, you should start enjoying every second of your life. Instead of being constantly stressed out worrying about abandonment, people or life as a whole start savoring every little moment.

The life we have is a very short one. Spending most of it obsessing and worrying over things that are out of your control makes it a colossal waste.

To enjoy life, you have to accept both the good and bad things that occur. When you are armed with self-esteem and value yourself, you will be able to perceive things clearly and face the challenges confidently.

For achieving a balance in your feelings, you need to live in the moment, accept your strengths and weaknesses.

When you are not bogged down by worries, fears and problems, you will be able to face them with the thought that things are meant to happen and you have the mindset to face them.

If you do not believe in yourself, remember that you are responsible for your feelings and you can support yourself regardless of what you face.

Trusting yourself and focusing on your inner strength will help you stop the fear and start enjoying every second of your life.

Steps to enjoy every breathing moment

1. Be Healthy

Take care of your health as good health keeps discomfort, pain, time and money spent on treatment and other stressful issues at bay.

Staying healthy is not a difficult task. You have to just keep an eye on what you eat and stick to a specific exercise routine that keeps you fit.

Eat the right foods, stay hydrated and sleep well every single day. This will make you feel active, vibrant and geared up to face the challenges of your daily life.

2. Be conscious of your surroundings

The joy and happiness you feel can come from the interactions you have with your surroundings and the people around you.

Meet up with friends and make new friends as hanging out with friends will make your entire day wonderful. Be people centered and kind to others. This will bring you joy and happiness.

3. Be forgiving

Constant worry and anxiety about your mistakes will affect your productiveness at work. It will also rob you of your happiness.

Hating yourself can destroy any progress you have achieved at work and in your personal relationship.

While it is good to remember your mistakes and strive to not repeat them, do not dwell on them. Make the effort to work out the problems before they bring you down and move on.

4. Love what you do

When you love your work, it will not seem like a chore. You will love getting up every day in anticipation of doing work you enjoy.

If your career does not do this for you, find some hobby you love and do it in your free time. This will help you relax and destress after a long day at work.

5. Be flexible

Don't harbor grudges against people or spend your day sulking at others. Every single grudge you hold will take away a part of your joy and happiness.

Be flexible and learn to forgive and let go. By being free of grudges, you can have a clear mind to face the challenges of your day. There will be no emotional baggage to keep you from achieving what you want.

Avoid holding grudges or postponing things that need to be done today. Don't spend your day thinking of better days in the past or future.

Try focusing your daily efforts on enjoying the present. Take life as it comes and live it to the fullest. Feel happy, laugh and enjoy starting from today and keep stressful situations or things at bay.

A fruitful journey

Self-realization brings you several amazing benefits. It allows you to observe your emotions and helps you learn how to handle your anxiety, stress and fear. You will let go of your destructive feelings and become empowered.

It helps you find your value and inner goals by taking away the trivial and unimportant things in your life. You can reach your full potential when you are not held back by distractions. The increase in self-awareness, self-esteem and confidence wards off the worries, insecurities and depression you feel.

You will start accepting yourself and your place in the world. You can have a clear perspective of your emotions and express them clearly and confidently.

Forming deeper and healthy relationships will not be difficult. You will find that you are connecting to people and enjoying it rather than trying to impress them and failing at it. In short, self-realization keeps you in a safe space that you need for healing yourself and for growing.

And remember that self-realization is not an overnight process. It takes time to reach the stage where you can have your own space and value yourself.

You need to be patient and practice, and turn the practice into habit, if you want to reach your destination. When you do reach, you will find that it was an eventful and beneficial journey giving you control over your life. You can take the next step towards leading a self-confident and happy life.

PART IV: The Healing Phase: Post Codependency Healing

As you would have fathomed by now, codependency is a multifaceted issue. However, the main underlying factor here is you lose focus of yourself. You expend efforts towards others at the expense of your own needs.

When you are in a codependent relationship, you feel depressed and alone as you are afraid to be yourself. In your efforts to see to the needs of those around you, you leave very little time for yourself.

In such a state, reaching out for recovery and healing is a gargantuan task. This is because you have to realize that you need help in the first place. If your partner looks to you to satisfy his or her needs you feel that you are indispensable. This makes reaching out to recovery a difficult task.

Feel the pain

In most codependent relationships, the recovery process does not start until the pain becomes unbearable. Yes, pain is the prime reason that makes you look for change. You reach a point where you are ready to take the leap.

When you decide that enough is enough, there will be no more sacrifices for the sake of others, you are making a good start on recovery.

Disregarding your wishes or putting them last creates resentment that festers inside and if you are not careful, it can destroy you completely. So, give your needs the importance they deserve. Look at what you want, as *you matter*.

Learn to express yourself

When you are unable to speak out what you want from your partner, it can create a passive aggressive behavior.

When you hide your resentment, it will find an outlet in the form of hurtful or sarcastic words. Being silent can become too oppressive forcing you to explode and the play of emotions in such a state will not leave you room to speak rationally.

So, you need to learn how to speak out, if you feel your needs or wants are not met. This way you will not bottle it all up and lose it phenomenally destroying whatever good that was left in the relationship.

Be human

You cannot always multitask and juggle your tasks trying to solve problems for others.

Admit that it is not possible to do everything right.

Not admitting can put you under undue stress that will leave you exhausted and depressed trying to be there for everyone.

Be supportive

It is possible to offer your support without offering advice, even if you are frustrated about losing control.

When people face difficulties and talk about them, most of the time they want others to understand them and not fix them. This is why advice is not accepted by many.

Advice irritates people regardless of their age.

So, listen to what your partner is saying and be supportive instead of rushing to the rescue suggesting hundred different solutions to the issue.

Know your responsibilities

Detachment does not come easy for anyone, especially a codependent person. You need to let go of the need to control outcome of situations that you are not responsible for.

In case of your partner, you have to let them handle a situation as they deem fit. This can make you anxious but it has to be done, if you want to move on.

And learn to say 'no'. It makes you honest and avoids landing you deep in the resentment pit. This is the last but not least important of the steps you should take to heal.

For self-care, you need to know your boundaries and learn to say no. This makes you put your needs first, which is a big and positive step forward.

Chapter 1: Mind and Body Relaxing Exercises

Stress can make you more vulnerable when you are in a dysfunctional relationship like a codependent relationship.

The emotional burden you carry around can push you into deep depression and destructive behavior. It can suppress all your strong points. To prevent this from happening, you need to take care of your body and mind.

When you realize that it is not others you have to take care of first but your own self, you should find the ways and means to make that happen. And the first step is taking care of your body.

Have you had a health check up recently?

If not, it is high time you got on to that. Even if you do not have any obvious issues, a checkup will help clear any doubts regarding conditions like high blood pressure, diabetes and other systemic conditions. Since you have neglected yourself in your rush to take care of others, now is the time to take the necessary steps.

When you have done a health evaluation and necessary treatment or precautions, consider your diet.

Is your diet a healthy one?

Are you aware of the right foods that are nutritious and healthy for your body?

Take up a diet plan that suits you best. There are plenty of diet programs that are really good in helping you maintain the right balance. Choose a reliable diet program that not only teaches you to consume the right foods but also teaches you how to maintain good nutrition.

And make the changes in small steps instead of diving right in. Set small goals, like adding a vegetable to your daily diet or drinking 3 glasses of water more than what you normally do.

When you succeed in the small goals, you can step it up. It is not necessary to be perfect. You have to just start focusing on the right path.

Exercise daily

If you are not in the habit of exercising daily, make it a habit to do some sort of physical exercise such as walking, cycling, aerobics, Pilates, yoga, etc.

Or, take up a sport that you enjoy. Devote twenty to thirty minutes of a day, three to four times in a week. This will take care of your cardiovascular health.

Just like with the diet start setting aside ten minutes daily in the beginning and increase the time gradually.

With exercise, you not only get to improve your blood circulation, but also keep yourself relaxed and energetic. Further, exercise is something that you have full control over.

To make it a routine, you need to set certain boundaries. As you focus on your diet and exercise you will start feeling better. Try being nice to yourself as you deserve it.

Mind and Body Relaxing Exercises

Relaxing helps in relieving stress. It also eases your depression, sleep issues and anxiety. Relaxing calms body and mind. It makes you feel calm and your muscles feel more fluid and less tense.

Relaxing can be done in a variety of ways. While some focus on mind relaxation, others focus on your body. But in general, most of the relaxation methods work on body and mind. Here are few of them

Mind Relaxing Exercises

1. Take slow and deep breaths. Try breathing exercises as these help in relaxation.

How to do:

Here are steps to help you practice deep breathing:

- Sit in a comfortable position with your back erect. Rest a hand over your stomach and the other over the chest region.
- As you breathe in, the hand placed over your stomach should move outward and the other should remain as such.
- Now breathe out with your mouth pushing maximum air out as you contract the stomach muscles. The hand over your stomach should move inwards when you exhale, but the hand over your chest should remain as such.
- Repeat the above steps either in sitting or lying down position. You can even place a book over your stomach and observe it rising and falling as you inhale and exhale.

The benefit:

The above breathing method is also called belly breathing. It stimulates vagus nerve that extends throughout the body from the head to your colon. It triggers relaxation response and reduces blood pressure, heart rate and lowers your stress.

2. Meditation is another powerful relaxation technique. Body scan meditation helps you concentrate on your body.

How to do:

Begin with your toes and work upward. Instead of relaxing the muscles as in the breathing exercises, here you just focus on each body part and label the sensations you feel as either bad or good.

Here are the steps:

- Lie in a supine position. Keep your legs and arms in relaxed position with eyes closed or open. Concentrate on breathing for a couple of minutes to let yourself relax.

- Now focus on the right foot toes. Observe any sensation that you feel as you concentrate on breathing in and out. Imagine your breath moving to your toes. Focus on each area for about five or more seconds.
- Repeat the same for the sole region of the right foot. Then move to right ankle, calf, knee, thigh, hip and then shift to the left leg. Now move to your torso, lower back, abdomen, upper back, chest and shoulders.
- Once you complete this body scan, be in a relaxed state for a few minutes. Now slowly stretch if needed.

3. Guided imagery is a good way to feel relaxed and calm. Use scripts, audiotapes or get assistance from a teacher to help with the guided imagery.

Here is an example of visualization technique:

Think about a tranquil lake. Include maximum sensory information that you can from this image such as see the calm and blue water, listen to the birds chirping, smell the blossoming flowers, feel the cool water and taste the clean and fresh air.

When you visualize, you will start feeling your worries going away as you explore your visual image. This may make your lose track of your present and you may feel your limbs getting heavy or you may twitch or yawn, which are all normal responses that you need not worry about.

4. Soak in nice warm bath

5. Music is an excellent mind relaxing tool. Listen to music

6. If you like to write about your feelings start keeping a journal.

Body Relaxing Exercises

1. Take up yoga. There are plenty of videos and books that help you practice yoga at home. You can also attend yoga classes.

2. Progressive muscle relaxing process: This technique involves focusing on each muscle group in your body as you tense and relax them. This helps reduce tension in your muscles and anxiety.

This method helps, if you find it difficult falling asleep. As you relax your muscles, signals are sent to your brain that falling asleep is okay.

How to do:

- Begin with your feet. Work upwards until you reach your face.
- Wear loose clothes, remove footwear and sit or lie down in a comfortable position.
- Breathe in and out deeply for a two to three minutes
- Now focus on right foot and how it feels. Tense the muscles tightly and hold for 10 counts
- Relax the foot and focus on the tension easing and on how the foot feels loose and limp
- Relax for a moment and shift to the left foot. Follow the same steps as you did for the right one
- Continue focusing on all parts of the body contracting your muscles and relaxing them
- This may need practice as you have to just tense only the intended muscles at any given time.
- Take up a relaxing activity like walking or other activities that you enjoy and keep you in a good mood.

3. A massage or back rub also relaxes your muscles. The relaxing effects of a massage session at a health club or spa may be known to you. Massage helps relieve pain, reduces stress and tension in the muscles. You can also practice self-massage.

Massage yourself between chores on your couch or bed when you retire for the day. This will help you unwind and sleep better. Use scented lotion, aromatic oil etc. along with deep breathing method.

Use a combination of strokes like tapping with cupped palms or fingers or gentle chops using your hands. For muscle knots, apply fingertip pressure. Use long, gliding and light strokes for kneading the muscles.

Here are steps for head and neck massage:

- Begin by kneading muscles present in the back of your shoulders and neck. Drum quickly upwards and on the sides and back of the neck using a loose fist.
- With your thumbs, do tiny circles near the skull base and massage the entire scalp region using fingertips. Using tapping movement of fingers on your scalp all over.
- For the face use tiny circles with thumbs or your fingertips and focus on forehead, jaws and temples.
- For your nose and eyebrows, use middle finger for the massage.
- End the massage by closing your eyes, covering your face with hands cupping them and breathe in and out for some time.

4. Drink something warm such as herbal tea or milk and avoid adding caffeine or alcohol.

Before You Begin the Relaxation Practice

The above techniques are just a small example of the type of things you can do to relax yourself. Learning them is easy but what you need to remember is that they should be practiced regularly to get the full stress relief benefits they provide. Make sure you spend a minimum of 20 minutes per day for relaxation.

If you have a busy schedule, try to meditate when you are commuting via train or bus or during your lunchbreak. Practice mindful walking when you exercise your dog.

Use your smartphone to view the relaxation guides available online. There are apps that you can use that guide you through the exercises, help you follow a proper routine and track your progress.

There will definitely be some hiccups as you try to stick to a proper schedule. Don't be discouraged. Even if there is a break of a few days or weeks, start again and build the momentum.

Chapter 2: Self-Confidence Boosting Efforts You Should Consider

Breaking free of codependency is a rough and uphill journey, but not an impossible one. Once you accept your codependent state and look for ways to break free you will find numerous pathways open to you.

The mind and body relaxing exercises mentioned above help you relax and view your situation objectively. The next step is gaining self confidence so you will feel capable of going the full length and face challenges courageously.

While self esteem is how you feel about yourself and love yourself and is developed by your experience and your growing environment, self confidence denotes the skills you develop to give you courage to handle any type of situation.

You need self-confidence to be free of your codependent state. With self-confidence, you can be successful in breaking free of codependent relationship and forge good relationships personally and professionally.

So here are a few efforts that help you boost your self-confidence.

Don't compare

Comparing your situations to others will make you envy them, which will make you feel worse about yourselves. This can turn into a vicious cycle.

No two individuals are the same and so are the situations you face. You need to stop comparing to look ahead, failing which you will be in danger of being trapped forever in a codependent relationship

Be healthy and fit

A fit body will keep your mind working in excellent condition. If you neglect your health, you will not feel good. Unhealthy diet, no exercise and very little sleep can take a huge toll on your health.

So, make sure you spend a few minutes every day on physical activity. This will help in boosting confidence. When you are physically fit you will feel more confident.

Self-compassion

Self-compassion entails being kind towards yourself. It is normal to feel anxious, depressed and blaming yourself for the issues you face in a codependent relationship. When you practice being compassionate towards yourself, you will start treating yourself with kindness.

It is human to err, so do not berate yourself whenever things go wrong.

Give breathing room to see the situation in a different perspective. Keep reminding yourself that being perfect is not as great as it is portrayed and that no one can be perfect.

Face your fears

If you have been putting off things due to fear of being rejected or rebuked or ignored, it is time you faced your fears.

You have fears such as these because you are not self-confident. Try facing the fears, even if the fear of embarrassment and failure deter you.

You need not be 100% confident to face your fears. Embrace your self-doubt, as this has proven to improve your performance.

Challenge your negative thoughts

When your mind prevents you from going forward with your self-care and confidence boosting efforts, you should tell yourself that such thoughts are not accurate.

The right way to deal with negative emotions and thoughts is to challenge them.

When you do so, you will find that anxiety or making a few errors do not end up as bad as you assumed. And with each positive step forward, you will find your confidence is largely improved.

Appreciate

The black spot in a white paper attracts more attention than the white background. This is true with our lives too. We are quick to identify the negativity in our lives, but fail to see the numerous positives present.

Learn to appreciate the good things in you. Focus on how these things have made you a better human being.

Appreciation helps eliminate the negativity. It gives you a realistic view where you can appreciate your strengths. You will feel happy and gain self confidence just by seeing what is already there in your life.

If you are feeling depressed, try finding something you have or someone in your life that you are grateful for.

You will find changes in your mindset and you will find more good things that bring happiness to you.

Work on your strengths

Self confidence will take a beating when you are unable to perform a task to the expected standards. All through your life you are bound to take up tasks that you cannot do well. This happens to everybody so you should not fret over it.

The problem with such tasks is when you spend more time on these tasks you struggle with them and this affects your confidence levels.

To boost self-confidence, you have to focus more on what you are good at. A successfully performed task will boost your confidence and you will feel as if you are an authority in that field. So, focus on things you are good at and spend time over them.

And for things that are not your strong points, don't spend excessive effort at being over competent except for the things that you are passionate about.

As I said before, perfection is an overrated concept. Instead of striving to be perfect in everything you do, keep building your strengths for better self-confidence.

Prepare yourself

Preparation is not only needed for the bigger things in life. Even your everyday tasks need preparation.

When you are prepared, you can do things better and this will incrementally add on leading to huge improvements in your work.

Being prepared will make you less afraid of the challenges you want to face in life. It helps in boosting your confidence.

If you want to confront your partner on an issue, think over it in advance so you can present your perspective in the proper way. This will prevent you from floundering at the first rebuttal from your partner.

Set goals and make plans to reach them

With purpose and direction in life, you will know you are moving in the right path. Setting goals help you to work towards achieving your objective in life.

The goals help you to work consistently and when you pass each milestone you will see progress. This boosts your self-confidence.

Progress denotes that you are reaching your goals continuously regardless of how trivial the goal is. Even a tiny little step forward should be seen as a big achievement and celebrated.

As you set goals and keep at them, you will find every day is just a step towards your destiny. You will feel more confident and happier about your progress.

Accept censure

Just as there is day and night, there are people around you who praise your efforts and others who are ready to disapprove every step you take.

Even if you bend backwards trying to please them, these people will not approve your efforts. And even if you please them, it is not you they are approving, but who you are impersonating.

Do not put too much value on the approval of others. This can end up in your sacrificing the goals, aspirations and dreams you have. This is actually a type of self-rejection, which can wreak havoc with your self-confidence.

Try to avoid seeking approval of those around you. You will feel free of the compelling and stressful need you have to get their approval. You will start behaving more naturally and realistically.

What you need to do is prove to yourself that you are a confident and skilled individual. If people around you do not realize this, you should ignore them as they are not worth your time.

Confidence issues are faced by everyone of us at some point in our life. But making it interfere with important things in your personal, social and work life can be detrimental to you.

At the same time, it is not good to be over confident. Placing overt confidence in your skills can prevent you from taking positive steps forward.

For instance, if you feel strong about your ability to score high marks in an upcoming test, you may not prepare for it. Hence take the effort to have the right dose of self confidence that will keep you performing well.

While the above measures help in boosting your self-confidence, in some cases there may be deep rooted issues that I have mentioned in the previous chapters. Growing up in a dysfunctional family can have long lasting impact on your mental health. In such cases, you may have to get professional aid to help you become more confident.

And remember that boosting self confidence is not an overnight task. You have to spend time, effort and concentration. Learned behaviors help you increase self-confidence. With healthy self-confidence levels, you can live a happy, healthy and motivated life.

The above measures are sure to help you move on to the next level. And since you deserve to live a life of happiness and joy, have faith, choose from the steps above and begin your first baby steps now and the joy you seek will be nearer than you imagined.

Chapter 3: Seek Support

When you are in a codependent relationship, you are isolated from your family, friends and social circle. Recovery can happen only when you step out and seek support from your family, friends and also from professionals.

But this is not an easy thing to do, especially if there is addiction involved. The fear and shame can keep you from seeking help.

An abusive relationship will have the abuser wielding control over your actions and interactions. They will cut you off from outside influence. I had experienced this with my controlling husband.

However, you should develop self esteem and confidence to ignore the fear and distrust. This will help you wake up and avoid attaching yourself to the negative thoughts of your partner.

Here are some ways in which you can seek support for codependency. You can choose any or all of these support measures to help you overcome your toxic relationship issues.

Why Support Is Key to Codependency Recovery

It takes tremendous effort on your part to achieve the self-discipline and focus to avoid being distracted or dissuaded from your efforts.

If the recovery efforts outlined in the previous chapters are not working for you, support is absolutely necessary.

It is also needed to sustain the efforts you have taken towards freeing from your codependent state.

Support will also help you focus on your objectives and help you move in the right direction.

And remember that you have to encounter plenty of discomfort as you face changes in your life such as new outlook of your personality, your fear of people or circumstances, incompetence and confusion in facing issues and more.

Awkward, guilty and anxious feelings are natural in this situation, which can drag you back to your old unhealthy habits. With continuous and staunch support, you can avoid this.

Support can be in the form of

1. 12 step Meetings
2. Psychotherapy

The comprehensive 12 step support program

The main purpose of this program is to offer a comprehensive support. It helps you accept that you have an issue, helps you face it and find the methods that can treat and heal it. The meetings are of four types:

1. Speaker meetings: These have a single person sharing his or her experience on codependency. The person may be undergoing recovery or fully recovered and offering help to others.

2. Topic share: These meetings involved different facets of addiction recovery. The leader of the group discusses about the 12 steps or gives information related to sponsorship.

3. Open Share: In open share type of meetings, every attendee will be given a chance to share his or her experience on overcoming codependency or on the hurdles they faced in recovery

4. Tradition study: Such meetings focus on the entire codependent recovery program and help codependents take the measures needed to help themselves.

The 12 steps of the program include:

1. Admit that you are powerless over others and that your life is not under your control
2. You believe that you are in need of a greater power to restore your sanity

3. Make a decision to turn your life and will to God's care
4. Make a fearless and searching inventory of yourself
5. Admit truthfully to your faults
6. Gear yourself to allow removal of your character defects
7. Seek help from God to overcome your shortcomings
8. Write a list of persons you have been hurtful and your willingness to make the necessary amends
9. Make the necessary amends as far as possible provided it does not affect others
10. Continue taking a personal inventory on your wrongs and admit to it
11. Use meditation and prayer to gain the knowledge and power to recover from the program
12. Experience spiritual awakening and help other codependents in their recovery process and practice the principles in all your efforts

Benefits of the program

Irrespective of the type of meeting you attend you can gain benefits such as

- Receive information from members with long time experience and also from books that are customized to your issues
- The meetings provide you with success stories and lessons from previous experiences and positivity of other members
- You can share your experience with other understanding people, get support and guidance via telephone or online meetings and also call a sponsor for support and advice between the meetings
- Keep yourself motivated and encouraged so you can continue with the recovery and healing process
- Attend meetings that are private and anonymous
- The spiritual addition in the meetings help you recover more effectively

- Daily meetings are held and you can choose a time that is convenient for you

Psychotherapy

This is a support system that is offered by a professional licensed in providing mental health support for codependency. The professionals include family and marriage therapists, clinical counselors and social workers who possess doctorates or master's degree in their specialty. The professionals help with prescription and also perform psychoanalysis, if it is a psychoanalyst.

Advantages of psychotherapy include

- Individual consultations that help address your specific issues.
- Objective and expert guidance that focuses on your specific issues, reactions, thought patterns and behavior, and suggest new and healthy patterns
- The personal therapy sessions help improve your intimacy skills
- For individuals uncomfortable with group meetings, the one to one guidance of psychotherapy sessions offers better confidentiality.
- Deep seated issues such as dysfunctional family, trauma, abuse, low self-esteem, shame, depression can be treated effectively by a professional
- The counseling therapy sessions gives an opportunity to work out issues you have with your spouse such as communication, parenting, sexuality and intimacy.

Regardless of the type of therapy you prefer, the support you get from people who have experienced codependency will be the best.

Family and friends can also pitch in, but they do not have the perspective needed or may be the reason for your problem. Thus, they can further worsen your denial, shame, fear and other issues you are fighting hard to get rid of.

Conclusion

"Incredible change happens in your life when you decide to take control of what you do have power over instead of craving control over what you don't." — **Steve Maraboli, Life, the Truth, and Being Free**

Unhealthy behavior can be recognized and changed, if you set your mind to it. One effective way to accomplish this is it educate yourselves on the various facets of a codependent relationship and how it impacts your life.

By now you would have realized that there is plenty of change and development needed for a codependent and those around the person including the spouse and other family members.

The caretaking behavior that you exhibit as a codependent allows the abuse to continue unhindered. You need to recognize codependent behavior to stop the abuse. And not only do you need to identify the behavior but also accept your needs and feelings.

And learning the power of no is one huge progressive step you can take that can lead you on to the path of self-reliance. When you manage to achieve this mammoth feat you will find love, serenity and freedom to live your life as you deem fit.

Learning more about your condition will help you grasp the minute nuances of the unhealthy and dysfunctional relationship. As you understand your situation better, you will be able to cope with the impact created by the unhealthy relationship.

And do not shy away from reaching out for assistance and support. If your codependency stems from childhood trauma, the treatment includes exploring childhood problems and relating them to your present destructive habits.

Try educating yourself on codependency and recovery. Take help from group and individual therapy sessions, and experiential groups.

Treatment also concentrates on helping you get in touch with your feelings, which you have suppressed during your childhood. The reconstructing of family dynamics with the help of therapy will help you connect with your feelings effectively.

It is not your fault

One crucial thing you have to understand about codependency is that it is not your fault. But you need to take responsibility to care for yourself to enable recovery. This will help you connect with your friends and family again.

Here are a few things that I have tried and found success, which I believe would benefit you immensely:

Be positive: Understand that being useful or always sacrificing yourself does not measure your worth. You deserve kindness and love as much as others

Practice prioritizing: Don't spend your waking hours seeing to the needs and satisfaction of others around you. The one person that deserves your whole attention and efforts is yourself.

Take part in fun activities: Allot time for fun activities with your friends. Make it a habit to share positive vibes and happy experiences with people other than your partner.

Cede control: You need not control everything around you. It is not possible to fix everything. Let some things be as they are.

Recover, heal and be happy: Be willing to expend effort, time, energy, care and commitment towards recovery. Join support groups or get help from psychotherapy to set healthy boundaries and heal from the codependency.

Light at the end of the tunnel

After having suffered from toxic behavior for several years, I was able to see a way out with my perseverance and support from friends, family and therapy. Just as I recovered from my harrowing experience, I trust that every individual suffering from codependency has the opportunity and ability to heal.

So, learn to let go, embrace self-esteem, think positive thoughts and gain confidence in your ability to live independently and fearlessly. Sacrificing your time, growth and efforts should never be a one-sided effort.

If this is how your relationship is, you have to consider making the necessary changes to bring back the relationship to an even footing. Or, take the efforts needed to free yourself from the sacrificial web you are caught in.

Set healthy boundaries, learn self-care and self-value and you will see a whole new world waiting for you. After all you deserve to be happy, content and loved just as every human being on this earth.

Best of luck.

If you liked this book let me know what you think, if you can find a time to leave an honest review on Amazon, I would appreciate it. Thank you

References:

https://www.passiton.com/inspirational-quotes/7692-you-yourself-as-much-as-anybody-in-the-entire

http://www.webster.edu/student-counseling/problems/codependent.html

https://www.goodreads.com/quotes/319248-incredible-change-happens-in-your-life-when-you-decide-to

Made in the USA
Las Vegas, NV
05 January 2021

15253886R00066